Meet the Press

Reading skills for upper-intermediate and more advanced students

Janice Abbott

Cambridge University Press
Cambridge
London   New York   New Rochelle
Melbourne   Sydney

For Jean-Claude

Published by the Press Syndicate of the University of Cambridge
The Pitt Building, Trumpington Street, Cambridge CB2 1RP
32 East 57th Street, New York, NY 10022, USA
296 Beaconsfield Parade, Middle Park, Melbourne 3206, Australia

First published 1981

Typeset by Keyspools Ltd, Golborne Lancs
Printed in Hong Kong by Wing King Tong Company Limited

ISBN 0 521 23286 4

Contents

To the student   1
To the teacher   4

1   News in brief   6

2   Home news   12

3   Foreign news   16

4   Business news   24

5   Technology and science   34

6   Comment   41

7   Letters to the editor   45

8   Motoring news   50

9   Travel news   58

10   Television   64

11   The arts   76

12   Sport   84

13   Advertisements   87

14   Features   96

Reading skills   99
Skimming
Scanning
Reading for the central ideas
Guessing the meaning of words

Headlines   102
The structure of headlines
The vocabulary of headlines

Advertisement abbreviations   105
Property advertisements
Entertainment advertisements

Answers   106

Acknowledgements

The author would especially like to thank Michael Swan, Barbara Thomas and Catherine Walter for the enormous amount of help and encouragement they gave while the book was being written and edited. The author would also like to thank Mario Rinvolucri for his initial enthusiasm and suggestions, and Rhian Jones, Diann Gruber and Vivian Dunne for their help.

The author and publishers are grateful to the newspapers, magazines, press agencies and individuals who have given permission for the use of copyright material. (Those sources which have not been identified in the text are given here.)
Extracts are from: The Associated Press, *Daily Mirror* (pp. 73–E,F; 75–M), *Daily Star* (pp. 72–A,B; 74–G,H), *The Daily Telegraph, Financial Times, The Guardian* (pp. 39–E; 40–F; 59–D), *The Houston Post* (© 1978 *The Houston Post*, reprinted by permission), *International Herald Tribune* (pp. 38–A; 51–F), London Express News and Feature Services – *Daily Express* (pp. 12–A; 59–B,E; 68–A), *Evening Standard* (pp. 9–G; 13–F), *The Sun* (pp. 72–C; 75–K, cartoon; 91–A) –, *Newsweek* (© 1978, 1979 Newsweek, Inc.), *The New York Times* (© 1979 by The New York Times Company, reprinted by permission, p. 15–A), *The Observer* (pp. 38–B; 39–C; 77–B), *Punch* (reproduced by permission), Reuters. *Time* (by permission of Time Magazine, the Weekly News Magazine © Time Inc., 1979), *The Times*, United Press International, *The Wall Street Journal* (reprinted by permission of *The Wall Street Journal* © Dow Jones and Company, Inc., 1979), *The Washington Post* (copyright) and individuals identified in the text.

It has not been possible to identify the sources of all material used and in such cases the publishers would welcome information from copyright owners.

Book designed by Peter Ducker

To the student

About the book

This book is a collection of newspaper extracts taken from all sections of mainly British and American newspapers and news magazines, with accompanying exercises designed to improve your reading skills. You may already have tried to read British or American newspapers and found that you quickly get bored and frustrated because the headlines are difficult to decipher and the articles long and complicated. This book aims to help you with the problems that make newspapers difficult to read and to encourage you generally to read faster and more efficiently.

The book is divided into 14 units. Each unit corresponds to a section or page in a newspaper and the order of the units roughly follows that of most daily newspapers. Each unit contains exercises to improve your reading skills. Emphasis has been placed on the skills which are useful for newspaper reading – scanning (reading quickly to find specific information), skimming (reading to identify the subject matter), finding the central ideas of a passage, guessing the meaning of words, and understanding newspaper headlines. A few exercises practise detailed comprehension. Most units also contain follow-up exercises which are aimed at improving your speaking and writing.

At the back of the book you will find a series of notes designed to help you when working through the exercises. There is a description of the reading skills, including advice on how to do the exercises in the book, an analysis of the special structure and vocabulary of newspaper headlines, a list of headline words, and a list of abbreviations used in advertisements. On page 101 there is a table indicating the different reading skills and the follow-up exercises practised, and where in the book to find them.

How to use the book

You may wish to work through the book unit by unit practising a variety of reading skills or you may prefer to concentrate on one reading skill at a time.

– Unit by unit. The units are not graded in difficulty, and with the possible exception of units 1 and 2 you can study them in any order. You should study units 1 and 2 first, because an understanding of the special vocabulary and structure of headlines, which is introduced and practised in these units, will help you in understanding the units which follow.

– Studying one reading skill at a time. In this case you should use the table on page 101. It is not necessary to complete all the exercises for each reading skill. Choose those articles whose subject matter interests you.

1

How to use the notes on reading skills

Whichever system you choose, remember to read the relevant section of the notes at the back of the book before attempting any of the reading skills for the first time. Suppose for example you wish to try Unit 1, Section B, Exercise 1. The exercise is to practise scanning, so before trying the exercise read carefully the section at the back of the book which explains scanning and gives you advice on how to tackle scanning exercises. The symbol ⇒ followed by a page number tells you which page to turn to. When you do the exercise be very strict with yourself about timing. Use a watch and follow the instructions concerning timing. You may find an article particularly interesting and wish to read it in detail, but do this only after you have completed the exercise to time.

Newspapers use many expressions and vocabulary which are not commonly found elsewhere. Where these expressions are important for the understanding of the extract an explanation is given.

Newspapers – some information

Below are some brief facts about the newspapers from which articles have been taken for this book.

British newspapers

The Daily Telegraph, Financial Times, The Guardian and *The Times* are known as the 'quality' newspapers. They are serious, national, daily newspapers, appealing mainly to the upper and middle classes.
The Daily Telegraph is right-of-centre in its views and contains reports on national and international news as well as covering sports and other topics.
Financial Times contains a comprehensive coverage of industry, commerce and public affairs and is read mainly by professional and business people.
The Guardian is the only 'quality' newspaper with liberal/left-of-centre politics. As well as a wide coverage of news events, it also reports on social issues, the arts, education etc.
The Times takes a middle-of-the-road view, claiming to represent the views of the establishment and is especially well-known for its correspondence column.

Daily Express, Daily Mail, Daily Mirror, Daily Star and *The Sun* are popular, tabloid newspapers – they are smaller in size and contain more photographs. They are not so serious as the 'quality' newspapers and their stories sometimes tend to be sensational. They have a national daily circulation and appeal mainly to the working and middle classes.
Daily Mail and *Daily Express* take a right-of-centre viewpoint on most issues.
Daily Mirror usually supports the Labour party.
The Sun and *Daily Star* are well-known for their pin-ups. *The Sun* has a larger circulation than any other daily newspaper.

Evening Standard was a popular London evening paper with right-of-centre politics and was read mainly by people travelling home from work. It was amalgamated with *Evening News* to become *The New Standard*.

The Observer is a serious national Sunday newspaper, comprising several sections including a colour supplement and is read mainly by the professional middle classes.

American newspapers

The New York Times is a serious daily newspaper read on a national scale, reporting on the arts, food etc. as well as covering national and international news.

The Wall Street Journal is a business/investment daily newspaper but it also carries news of national importance.

The Washington Post is a serious daily newspaper which is of national interest, in particular because it contains full coverage of Congress.

The Houston Post is published in Houston, Texas.

Other newspapers

International Herald Tribune is a daily newspaper produced in Paris and sold in most countries of the world. It covers American and international news and contains advertisements and reviews. It is aimed at an international audience and is read by Americans living outside the USA in particular.

Magazines

Newsweek is a weekly American news magazine which covers American and international news and a wide range of topics. There is also an international edition.

Punch is a weekly British satirical magazine which is well-known for its cartoons.

Time magazine is sold all over the world and contains articles on US and world news as well as general articles on culture, medicine etc.

New organisations

Most newspapers contain reports by news organisations. Some of the articles in this book are reports by the Associated Press, Reuters or United Press International. The Associated Press has staff reporters, editors and photographers in 60 foreign countries and 107 US cities who send news and photographs to all parts of the world. Reuters gathers, edits and distributes news to the media and the business communities in 159 countries.

To the teacher

Content and aims

Designed for upper-intermediate and more advanced students of English, this book brings together a selection of extracts taken mainly from different British and American newspapers and news magazines. Advertisements, cartoons, book and theatre reviews are included as well as news articles. The extracts have been printed as they originally appeared in each newspaper.

The book is for people who wish to improve their reading skills in English, particularly those reading skills necessary for understanding newspapers. The exercises accompanying the extracts teach and practise the general reading skills of skimming, scanning, finding the central idea, guessing the meaning of words and detailed comprehension, as well as the special reading skill of understanding the structure and lexis of newspaper headlines. Follow-up exercises use the extracts as a stimulus for language activities other than reading – role-play, writing and discussion.

The book is divided into 14 units. Each unit corresponds to a section or page in a newspaper and the order of the units roughly follows that of most daily newspapers. At the back of the book there is a table listing the different reading skills and follow-up exercises practised, and showing where in the book to find them. There is also a description of the reading skills, including advice on how to do the exercises in the book, an analysis of the special structure and vocabulary of newspaper headlines, a list of headline vocabulary, and a list of abbreviations used in advertisements.

How to use the book

One way of using the book is to work through unit by unit giving your students practice in all the different reading skills as well as the writing and speaking activities. The units are not graded in difficulty, and with the possible exception of units 1 and 2 can be dealt with in any order. It is advisable to cover units 1 and 2 first, because an understanding of the special vocabulary and structure of headlines, which is introduced and practised in these two units, will help students in studying the units which follow.

The units vary considerably both in length and in the kinds of reading skills and other activities practised. Each unit is divided into a number of sections. The length of time needed to cover any one section will obviously vary according to the length of the section, to the speed at which different groups work and to the reading skills and other activities practised in the section. It is probably not a good idea to cover more than one section in any one teaching session, and in some cases it may be necessary to spend more than one teaching session on a section.

An alternative way of using the book is to study one reading skill at a time. You may wish, for example, to concentrate on skimming, then on scanning etc. In this case you will find the table on page 101 essential.

When doing the exercises, stretch your students. Give them a strict time limit and keep to it. Many students read slowly and inefficiently because they have never been encouraged to read faster.

Newspapers use many expressions and vocabulary which are not commonly found elsewhere. Where these expressions are important for the understanding of the text an explanation is given. It is important to warn students not to use the more 'journalese' expressions in their own speaking or writing.

How to use the notes on reading skills

Whichever way you decide to work through the book, it is important to make use of the notes at the back of the book. Suppose for example that you want to use one of the exercises practising scanning. First read the section on page 99 which explains what is involved in scanning. You can then convey this information to the students either by explaining it directly yourself or by asking the students to read the section themselves. Even if you decide to explain the reading skill yourself ask the students to read the description afterwards (perhaps as homework). It is important that the students are familiar with the notes and word lists at the end of the book, so that they can refer to them as they work through the book.

They are reminded to do this by the symbol ⇒ followed by a page reference which refers to the section at the back of the book which is relevant to that particular exercise.

NEWS IN BRIEF

Section A

1 Below you will find a set of twelve headlines taken from British and American newspapers. Following these are the articles which appeared with the headlines. Match the headlines and the articles. ⇒ page 99–A.

¹ Come back Legionnaire

² Cannabis haul

³ Shirley's pledge on crowded classes

⁴ Custody rule

⁵ *Boost for jobless*

⁶ Plea for newsmen

⁷ MORE JOBS FOR BLACKS PLEDGE BY CARTER

⁸ Girls die in blaze

⁹ Papers hit again

¹⁰ CRASH DRIVER TURNS WHITE

¹¹ CAT DODGERS' FINE .. £1,500

¹² Gypsy status

A

THE INTERNATIONAL Gypsy organisation has applied for UN consultative status, Romani Union president Jan Cibula announced yesterday. Mr Cibula and 12 delegates representing gypsy groups from several countries will meet for six days of talks at the UN's New York headquarters at the end of February.— UPI.

UN: United Nations

B

CUSTOMS officers at Heathrow airport seized cannabis worth £2,500 yesterday after questioning a man and two women who had arrived from Kingston, Jamaica. The drugs were hidden in two suitcases.

C THE Liverpool Daily Post did not appear again this morning because of an industrial dispute, a company spokesman said, and it was unlikely that the Liverpool Echo, which is also affected, would produce an evening edition. But there had been some progress towards a settlement in weekend talks between the management and the National Graphical Association, the spokesman added.

D When student Roderic Morrison, 21, of Peterhead, Grampian, received a letter from Dundee University telling him he had failed his medical exams, he left home, travelled to Paris and signed on for five years in the Foreign Legion.

But now his worried parents have received a letter offering him a place at an Aberdeen college to study for a chemistry degree. Yesterday his mother, Mrs Jane Morrison, said she and her husband had approached the Foreign Office and would ' leave no stone unturned ' to get Roderic home.

Foreign Legion: part of the French army noted for strict discipline
leave no stone unturned: do everything possible

E A driver emerged dazed, shaken and white—from head to foot—after his van careered out of control and somersaulted three times yesterday. The lid of a gallon tin of paint had flown off in the crash, showering him in brilliant white emulsion.

Mr Gary Glover, the driver, of Maytree Crescent, North Watford, Herts, had hit a patch of oil at the William Street roundabout, Slough.

F L O C A L authorities have been warned by the Government not to save money on schools by cutting the ratio of teachers to children.

Education Minister Shirley Williams told a Harrogate conference yesterday that she had been forced to shut teacher training colleges to prevent teachers going on the employment scrap-heap.

But she said the Government planned to improve the teacher ratio even if the birth rate stopped falling.

Mrs. Williams made an obvious reference to the situation at Stockport, Cheshire, and Oldham, Lancs, where teachers have refused to take " overcrowded " classes.

She said : " I know that some authorities are ignoring my advice."

G PLANS to cut the dole queue were announced in the Commons last night by Employment Secretary Albert Booth.

He said the Government subsidy given to small firms which take on extra workers in job black spots is to be extended to cover the whole country.

On top of this, the deadline for applications to join the scheme is to be extended to March, 1980.

the dole: money British people receive from the state while they are out of work

H A TAIWANESE freighter captain who brought almost 3,400 Vietnamese refugees to Hong Kong aboard his ship, the Huey Fong, was remanded in custody for one week when he made a second appearance in court yesterday. Shu Hsin-wen, aged 52, is charged under Hong Kong laws against refugee trafficking and could face a four-year prison term. — Reuter.

remanded in custody: kept under arrest

I SOUTH AFRICA was yesterday called on to charge four journalists being held in detention or else release them. The demand was made by the South African Society of Journalists. It claimed that in the past year 50 journalists had been affected by government bannings and other actions.

J TWO girls aged 18 and 17 died in a blaze today at the terrace house they shared with three young men in Alton Road, Tuesbrook, Liverpool.

K President Carter met Black Congressional leaders yesterday to promise them he will give higher priority to tackling the problem of fast-rising unemployment among Black people.

He has lately been under increasingly bitter attack from Black spokesmen for taking the Black vote, which was solidly behind him, too much for granted and failing to attend to their needs.

Mr Carter agreed that the jobless figures for last month were " horrible " and said there had to be more " Government-sponsored employment opportunities." Among Black youths unemployment is now 40 per cent.

L THREE French tourists, who smuggled two cats into Britain in their car, were each fined £500 under the anti-rabies laws yesterday. But the tourists had only £102 on them when they were arrested. Now they face thirty days in jail unless the French Consul agrees to pay the balance of the fine to magistrates at Maidstone, Kent.

2 Choose one of the articles and read it carefully. Prepare to give the rest of the class a summary of the article.

3 What is the meaning of the following words in the headlines in which they appear?
hit
haul
pledge
blaze
plea
Why do you think the headline writer chose the above words, rather than the words you have given as being similar in meaning?
⇒ A number of words which are not so common in everyday language appear very frequently in headlines. A knowledge of these words makes the understanding of headlines much easier. On page 103 you will find a list of words which either tend to occur in headlines more often than elsewhere, or occur in special senses which they do not have in ordinary language.

4 Rewrite the following headlines, replacing the underlined words with the correct form of words from this list: attempt, exceed, conquer, dispute, affect, marry, request, forbid, seize.

¹ Job <u>row</u> may <u>hit</u> children's hospital

² Crime profit tops £166m

³ Mother's <u>plea</u> for son fails

⁴ Young wife's <u>bid</u> to <u>beat</u> fear

⁵ Bus <u>ban</u> on pupils after attack on crew

⁶ Actress <u>weds</u>

⁷ £1 million heroin <u>haul</u>

5 Choose two of the headlines from exercise 4 and write a short article to go with each of them. When you have finished, read out your article to the rest of the class and see if they can guess which headline you chose.

6 Below you will find the articles which appeared with the headlines shown in exercise 5. Match the articles and the headlines. ⇒ page 99–A

A

A MOTHER'S plea that she should not be separated from her young son during his formative years failed at Inner London Crown court last week when her appeal against a six-month jail sentence for theft was dismissed.

Vivienne Pottinger (22), of 6 Loanda House, Linden-grove, Peckham, had been sentenced at Camberwell for theft, dishonest handling and deception. A six-month suspended sentence had also been brought into effect, meaning she would serve a year in jail.

Defence counsel said her son was born while she had been in Borstal for shoplifting and it would be undesirable for her to be separated from him during his formative years. She was worried that she would have no home to go to when she was released. She was appealing on the grounds that the sentence was excessive.

Prosecution said she had a record of theft. On July 8 police visited her home and found a TV set which she admitted she obtained from a rental company and then moved without paying.

They also found correspondence relating to Whitney blankets, valued at £96, which she had obtained in a similar way, and two record players which she had every reason to believe were stolen.

The court dismissed the appeal.

Inner London Crown Court: Court of Justice
Borstal: reform school for young offenders

B

Busmen refused to carry pupils of a London comprehensive school yesterday after an inspector had nearly lost an eye and three other busmen had been injured when schoolchildren attacked a bus crew.

Crews imposed a ban on pupils of Kingsdale School in Alleyn Park, Dulwich, where a pupil, thought to have started the incident, has been suspended.

About 18 pupils turned on a conductor on Monday after he had told a youth to stop smoking on the lower deck of a bus.

C

THE FORMER Swedish Liberal Party leader and Deputy Prime Minister, Mr Per Ahlmark, has married the actress Bibi Andersson—best known for her roles in Ingmar Bergman's films. Miss Andersson, 43, rose to fame in 1957 with her role in Bergman's The Seventh Seal and has since belonged to the group of actors favoured by the Swedish director.— UPI.

D HEROIN worth more than £1 million was distributed by accident in packets of frozen prawns delivered to Chinese restaurants in Glasgow after a ship from Hong Kong docked at Newcastle. Police have recovered most of the consignment and have launched a full-scale investigation.

E

THE country's leading children's hospital, Great Ormond Street, in London, is facing industrial action by more than 160 domestic staff.

The staff—members of four unions—are annoyed at the hospital Governors' decision to place the domestic department under a manager from an outside contract cleaning firm.

They say the job should have gone to someone already in the hospital service or from another hospital, and have threatened to take action tomorrow unless the appointment is cancelled.

Shop stewards will be meeting management today to try to resolve the row which could affect more than 270 children at the London hospital.

Hospital Secretary Mr Austin Lyth said last night that he had not been told what form the industrial action might take.

F NEW crime figures yesterday shocked police chiefs who thought they were winning the war against thieves.

Crooks netted £166,850,000 in Britain last year.

The figures, in the Security Gazette, are merely the tip of the criminal iceberg.

For they do not include losses from fraud, forgery, embezzlement or the hundreds of millions in goods stolen by shoplifters each year.

The £166 million is also clear, criminal profit, for the figures take no account of the £31 million in cash and valuables recovered.

But in a speech in Sussex last night, Commissioner Sir David "Hammer" McNee said that his force, under-manned at the same level it was in 1921, faced an acute crisis in London.

G

A RADICAL new group is being started in London to help people with agoraphobia—a dread of open spaces.

A young housewife is arranging a meeting for sufferers at her home in Tabley Road, Holloway — which they will have to leave home to attend.

Mary Husseyin, 20, an agoraphobic for two years, believes the only way to beat the illness is to fight it. Recently she proved her point by going out shopping with her husband.

"It was terrible," she said. "I panicked. I cannot remember having been so terrified.

"The people, the cars, the traffic made me feel as if my head would burst. But I stood there thinking: Well, it cannot kill me. And after a while it went away and I wanted to stay out. I really enjoyed it."

Mrs Husseyin, whose marriage has been threatened by her illness, thinks that other agora phobics can make the same progress. She is calling a meeting so that sufferers will have an incentive to get out and attend.

Her telephone number is 609 3558 and her address is 19 Tabley Road, N.7.

tip of the iceberg: a very small part of the problem

9

1 Below and on page 11 you will find a number of short articles. Your objective in this exercise is to scan the articles quickly for certain information. Do not worry about detail that is not directly related to the information you are looking for. Do not attempt to understand each article completely. Simply look for the information you are required to find.   ⇒ page 99–B.

   a) Which country is having a Courtesy Campaign?
   b) Why did a South African soldier kill two men?
   c) Who made a speech in New York?
   d) Where did a boat capsize yesterday?
   e) What is Mrs Tom Claire's job?
   f) Which institution conducted the study in contraceptives?
   g) How long is the block of ice from Antarctica?
   h) How many householders are receiving free solar heating?
   i) What is the NRC?

2 Below you will find statements about the information contained in the articles you have just read. Decide whether the statements are true or false. If a statement is false, correct it. You will need to read the articles in more detail to do this exercise.

   a) Edward Kennedy has been campaigning for harsher punishment of juvenile crime for many years.
   b) The householders receiving free solar heating will have to return the solar collectors at the end of the research project.
   c) The Vietnamese refugees died when Malaysian villagers fired at them.
   d) Stefanus van der Merwe was found not guilty of the murder of two men.
   e) Five atomic power plants will be closed because of the enormous cost to the country.
   f) A column of ice will be used to study the weather conditions of the last 2,500 years.
   g) The stamps showing a sculpture of the baby Jesus were part of a special issue to celebrate the Year of the Child.

A U.S. Shuts Down 5 Nuclear Plants For Quake Faults

WASHINGTON, March 13 (UPI) — The Nuclear Regulatory Commission today ordered five atomic power plants shut down immediately because their cooling systems may be unable to withstand earthquakes.

In an action with potentially large implications for U.S. energy supplies, the NRC said that an improper computer formula used to design the plants more than seven years ago led to inadequate support for cooling system pipes. If the pipes failed, it said, two of the three main lines of defense against major reactor accidents could be breached.

B 140 DROWNED AS VIET BOAT SINKS

ABOUT 140 Vietnamese refugees were feared drowned yesterday when their boat capsized in heavy seas off north-east Malaysia.

Angry villagers had refused to let them land and pushed the boat back in the sea.

C

Courtesy song

THE music makers in the Singapore Police Force have added a jaunty tempo to the National Courtesy Campaign.

They have composed a bright and catchy tune, Courtesy Should be Shining through the Heart, to mark the campaign. Set to the tempo of a march, it was sung for the first time at the Police Academy yesterday.

D

The Ice Cometh To Leningrad

MOSCOW, March 13 (UPI) — Soviet explorers have cut a column of ice 130 meters long from Antarctica and plan to ship it to Leningrad, where it will be studied, Tass reported

Scientists believe that the column will provide a "frozen annal" of weather and climate conditions for the last 2,500 years, according to the report.

E

FREE SOLAR HEAT PLAN

Free solar heating is being offered to 40 householders. The Building Societies research and information association wants to instal it in Lincolnshire as part of a Government research programme.

Solar collectors are to be installed on roofs and larger hot-water cylinders in airing cupboards. Householders may keep the equipment.

F

S. Africa Soldier Admits Killing 2 Blacks in Anger

KLERKSDORP, South Africa, March 7 (AP) — A cavalry instructor told a court today that he shot dead two black hitchhikers when they threw away cigarettes he gave them after just a few puffs.

The South African Press Association reported that Stefanus van der Merwe, 19, said: "At times I get so terribly cross, even at servicemen, that I feel I can drill them dead." The shootings occurred in November.

The judge declared him not guilty of murder by reason of insanity and committed him to a mental asylum, the agency said.

G

A Naked Jesus On U.S. Stamp Riles Women

GARDEN CITY, Kan., Dec. 7 (AP) — Three women here have complained that the U.S. Postal Service is selling what they term indecent material — Christmas commemorative stamps depicting an unswaddled baby Jesus.

The stamp depicts a sculpture by 15th-century artist Andrea Della Robbia "Madonna and Child with Cherubim," which is at the National Gallery of Art in Washington.

Mrs. Tom Claire, a postal clerk, said that when a woman returned a roll of the stamps, "She asked me to look. I looked and I still didn't see anything. I looked again and she said the child wasn't clothed and that she wouldn't put the stamp on her cards."

Two more women separately returned the stamps complaining that they were indecent, Mrs. Claire said.

The women wanted their money back. They were given stamps depicting reindeer.

H

Contraceptives Lower Births For Teen-Agers

WASHINGTON, June 19 (UPI) — A nationwide survey shows contraceptives prevented about 680,000 pregnancies among unwed teen-age girls during a one-year period, and more pregnancies could be prevented if contraceptives were more readily available.

The study, conducted by Johns Hopkins University sociologists Melvin Zelnik and John F. Kantner in 1976, also disputed the "widely held beliefs" that increased availability of contraceptives leads to widespread sexual activity and more abortions.

"If none of today's sexually active teens used birth control methods, the number of such pregnancies would be 1,460,000 each year instead of the 780,000 which actually occur," the authors said.

"Certainly, these findings leave no room for complacency . . . but they do show that many teen-agers are using contraception, are using effective methods, and are using them regularly," the sociologists said.

I

Hard line on crime

Youngsters who commit violent crimes should be treated as adults and sentenced to "significant punishment," Senator Edward Kennedy said in New York.

In a speech at the convention of the International Association of Chiefs of Police, he backed, for the first time, moves to try juveniles accused of violent crimes in adult courts.

unswaddled (Biblical word): unclothed

2

HOME NEWS

Section A

1 Look very quickly through the articles which follow. You only need to get a very general idea of the contents. Do not worry about detail or vocabulary you do not know. ⇒ page 99–A. Which of the articles might be of particular interest to the following people
   a) a deaf person?   c) a lorry driver?
   b) a football fan?   d) an animal lover?
   Which of the articles
   e) mention young people?   h) report something which is going to happen?
   f) report violence?   i) report something which happened in the past?
   g) deal with sport?

2 Below you will find statements about the information contained in the articles you have just read. Decide whether the statements are true or false. If a statement is false, correct it. You will need to read the articles in more detail to do this exercise.
   a) The BBC has invented a system which will help the deaf.
   b) The new TV sets for the deaf will be no more expensive than ordinary sets.
   c) The new TV sets for the deaf will help relations between deaf people and the general public.
   d) Mr Bates has been manager of the Water Garden Hotel for many years.
   e) The police arrested the two burglars at the Water Garden Hotel.
   f) When the raiders arrived Mr Bates was in the hotel lobby.
   g) MPs want to ban all lorries from Britain.
   h) Nottingham has a cockroach epidemic.
   i) The signalmen are striking for the right to make a cup of tea.
   j) Richard Gibbon's leg was amputated after he fell from a train.

A Soccer boy rail victim

DOCTORS yesterday won their fight to save the leg of a 16-year-old boy who fell from a train in an outburst of Soccer violence.

And after a night of anguish, waiting for news from the hospital, the boy's father, factory manager Mr Albert Gibbon, spoke bitterly of the thugs who are making the game too dangerous to attend.

At his home in Park Lane, Fareham, Mr Gibbon said: "My immediate reaction is to plead wth any parent that if they value their children's lives, don't send them to football matches.

"I used to be a Soccer fan myself but when I went to a game there was none of this violence."

Richard Gibbon, a keen Portsmouth supporter, had been to the "friendly" home match on Saturday between Portsmouth and Chelsea.

He was returning by train when fighting broke out. As the train approached Fareham station he and two other youths were seen to fall from a carriage.

Richards's leg was struck by a train wheel and at the Royal Portsmouth Hospital doctors feared at first they would have to amputate.

The other youths were also taken to hospital but were not seriously injured.

Earlier, at the Soccer ground, police with dogs broke up an invasion of the pitch and arrested 23 youths before the kick-off.

Thirty more were thrown out during the tense, rowdy, pre-season match.

Last night nine youths were charged with assault.

B TV TO AID THE DEAF

By LESLIE TOULSON

BBC experts have invented a new system that lets the deaf understand television programmes.

But sets capable of providing sub-titles for every programme will cost at least a third more than conventional ones, and the BBC hopes the Government will foot the bill.

Deaf viewers would be able to "dial" for sub-titles, to be provided by the BBC's Ceefax information line. This at present screens facts like share prices and race results.

Mr Bill Wood, the BBC's head of engineering information, said yesterday: "Deaf people cannot discuss programmes, and this is why many people treat the deaf as though they are stupid."

C Pet plan approved

A council yesterday gave a pet shop owner permission to breed from two giant African cockroaches

Health officials of Broxtowe District Council, Notts, ordered an investigation after a retired American professor had forecast that, should the insects escape, Nottingham would have a cockroach epidemic

But yesterday a council spokesman said: "They will not breed at below 60F, which means that, if any escape, one sharp frost and they will be wiped out.

A pet shop owner, Steve Zlotowitz, and his wife Carol, both 27, of Beeston, Notts, plan to sell the cockroaches as pets at £1.20 a pair.

D Storm in a tea cup

THOUSANDS of homeward-bound commuters were stranded in their train carriages yesterday evening when a signalman pressed his demand for a pay rise by stopping work to make a cup of tea.

Other railmen had caused similar delays earlier in the day

Three signalmen at Bethnal Green, London, are threatening further disruption unless their demands for regrading — and a £5-a-week pay rise—are met.

They are defying union instructions to work normally until the proper procedures have been exhausted. But the men, who each work eight-hour shifts, said they would continue to boil their kettle once every shift at the most inconvenient time

A British Rail spokesman said: "We don't really know what will happen. The first warning we get is when they ring up and say the kettle is boiling."

storm in a tea cup: great excitement over something trivial

E MPs to fight juggernaut lorries plan

ANGRY MPs will demand a statement on plans for heavier juggernaut lorries when Parliament re-opens today.

They are furious about a leaked report which claims that Department of Transport civil servants aim to raise the maximum gross weight of lorries in Britain from 32 tons to 38 or 40 tons.

F Hotel manager tricks gunman

PETER BATES talked his way out of trouble after two armed raiders burst into his flat and put a gun to his head today.

Mr Bates, working his first day as manager of a London hotel, convinced them he would have to go upstairs to get the keys for the safe.

And when the raiders let him go he rang the police from the hotel lobby.

But the men, one of them believed to be armed with a pistol, escaped by a fire-escape before the police arrived.

Record

"I thought my time was up when they put the gun to my head," said 28-year-old Mr Bates, manager of the Water Garden Hotel in Earls Court.

"I've only been manager here for one day. I hope it's not always like this."

The two men, one dressed in a white suit and the other all in black, were lying in wait for him in his basement flat at the hotel when he arrived home from a night out early today.

They made him put on a record at top volume. One punched him in the eye, pulled out a gun and took all the money from his pockets—£6.40.

Then they demanded the money from the hotel safe at the 55-bedroomed £14-a-night hotel.

"I thought I was dead," said Mr Bates. "I would have given them the money, I would not have risked my life or the night porter's.

"I told them the money was in the safe upstairs and they gave me three minutes to go and get it. They said they would send someone back to blow my head off if I didn't come back."

The robbers escaped after a burglar alarm went off.

It was not the only drama of Mr Bates' first night. Travellers cheques and a passport were taken from a room at the hotel.

1   Look carefully at the headlines of the articles you read in section A. Rewrite them as full sentences. Compare your sentences with the headlines and try to identify the differences.

⇒   Headlines are difficult to read not only because they use special vocabulary, but also because they have their own particular structure. Refer to page 102 before continuing with the following exercise.

2   Look at the following headlines. For each one, write down in a few sentences what you think the article which goes with it might be about.

1   # SOS from burglar stuck in chimney

2   # Dolphins to Join Loch Ness Hunt

3   # TRAFFIC WARDENS TAKE PAY ACTION

5   # Union chiefs pay probe

4   # Walk-off threat over dirty jets

6   # More steel jobs axed

3   On page 15 you will find the articles which appeared with the headlines shown above. Match the headlines and the articles.   ⇒ page 99–A.

4   Read article A carefully. Below are seven words and expressions taken from it. In each case decide which of the four alternatives following the word or expression is most similar in meaning to it in the context of the article.   ⇒ page 100–D.

a) *resume*
   i)   end
   ii) happen
   iii) create excitement
   iv) begin again

b) *enlist*
   i)   make a list of
   ii) demonstrate against
   iii) make use of
   iv) encourage

c) *falling into place*
   i)   going well
   ii) going wrong
   iii) disappearing
   iv) breaking

d) *survey*
   i)   investigate
   ii) swim through
   iii) photograph
   iv) penetrate

e) *track*
   i)   follow
   ii) attack
   iii) surround
   iv) fight

f) *under way*
   i)   below water
   ii) forbidden
   iii) in progress
   iv) coming to an end

g) *feasible*
   i)   dangerous
   ii) exciting
   iii) safe
   iv) possible

A The search for evidence of the legendary monster of Loch Ness will resume this summer and this time the searchers plan to enlist the services of dolphins to photograph any large creatures in the Scottish lake.

Dr. Robert H. Rines, the Boston patent attorney who has led expeditions to the lake each summer for a decade, said yesterday that "everything is falling into place" in preparation for using two camera-carrying dolphins to survey the deep waters. The dolphins have been in training all winter in Florida.

In all the tests thus far, Dr. Rines said in an interview, the animals have demonstrated that they had no trouble carrying cameras and strobe lights attached to shoulder harnesses or vests. They were able to find, track and photograph large underwater creatures such as sea turtles and sharks. In a few weeks the dolphins will begin a period of acclimation to colder water.

The expedition is sponsored by the Academy of Applied Science of Boston. A number of experts from the United States Navy's San Diego Research Center, where considerable experimentation with dolphins is under way, have been consulted in the care and training of dolphins for underwater exploration.

Dr. Rines said that Navy officials had assured him that the project was feasible and dolphin experts had assured him that it posed no threat to the animals' safety.

"The obvious problems of using the dolphins in fresh water and at relatively lower temperatures have received very careful attention," Dr, Rines said, "with unanimous agreement by our Navy and other institutions and other experimenters in this area that there is absolutely no danger or discomfort or strain on the dolphins in operating as we propose at Loch Ness."

Dr. Rines said that the dolphins had already had at least 20 continuous hours in fresh water. At Loch Ness they will be kept in salt-water holding tanks and released into the lake for a few hours of searching each day.

B The 1,000 traffic wardens in London decided yesterday to take industrial action over a pay claim. The wardens claim that the action could lead to massive traffic snarl-ups.

At a mass meeting at the Central Hall, Westminster, they decided by an overwhelming majority: To ban all overtime from Monday; to refuse to wind up any of London's meters—which means they will all be inoperative within 72 hours; and to ban all voluntary duties such as driving, follow-up inquiries, car pound duties and clerical work.

snarl-ups: bad traffic jams
car pound: enclosure for cars removed from road by police

C British Airways stewards and stewardesses protesting about dirty planes and faulty equipment say that from next Monday they will walk off any aircraft not 'in a satisfactory condition' — even if it means delays for passengers.

D IRON and steel making will cease at the Bilston plant in Staffordshire in April 1980 throwing 1,900 men on the dole queue.

And British Steel is cutting a further 1,700 jobs at Scunthorpe, Lincs.

As soon as they heard the news, workers at Bilston demanded a national strike to try and save their jobs, but it seems unlikely that the Iron and Steel Trades Confederation will agree.

E THREE cat burglars thought they had a good idea—climb down a chimney to get into a clothing store. The trouble was, the fireplace had been bricked up.

One of them found himself stuck at the bottom of a 15ft shaft. The others had to wave frantically from the rooftop until they caught the eye of a passing policeman.

Firemen had to break down the fireplace at Wakefield's Army store in the Market Place, Leicester.

Three men were later helping police

cat burglar: burglar who enters by climbing to upper floor

F THE Department of Employment is investigating bumper pay rises awarded to themselves by powerful union chiefs, it was revealed in the Commons yesterday. Among the 60 per cent increases under the scrutiny is a plan to raise T.U.C. General Secretary Mr Len Murray's salary from £9,000 to £16,000 by 1980.

bumper: big
TUC: Trades Union Congress

15

³ FOREIGN NEWS ▰▰▰▰

Section A

1   Look very quickly through the articles which follow. You only need to get a very general idea of the contents. Do not worry about detail or vocabulary you do not know.   ⇒ page 99–A. Which article(s) mentions something about
    a) the weather?   d) money?
    b) religion?   e) death?
    c) space travel?   f) the police?

2   Scan the same articles for the information required in the questions below. Do not worry about detail that is not directly related to the information you are looking for. Do not attempt to understand each article completely.   ⇒ page 99–B.
    a) Why was a whale sold to Hong Kong?
    b) How many people died in road accidents in Sweden in 1978?
    c) In which town does Professor Vladimir Dorofeyev work?
    d) Why was a man shot to death in New York?
    e) What was the highest temperature at the South Pole during April?
    f) Why did three women kill a policeman in San Salvador?
    g) How many cattle died as a result of the heavy rains in India?
    h) What did the box sent from Milan to Sardinia contain?
    i) Is Dr Barnard in favour of euthanasia?
    j) When was Pegasus 1, the American satellite, launched?
    k) For what purpose was Pegasus 1 launched?
    l) Who, according to tradition, was St Januarius?

3   Which article interests you most? Read it carefully to yourself working out the meaning of vocabulary that you do not know.   ⇒ page 100–D.

A

5 Die at Ganges River

NEW DELHI, Jan. 15 (AP).— Five persons were killed and 24 injured today when thousands of Hindu pilgrims stampeded into the holy Ganges River where it joins the Bay of Bengal at Sagar Island, the Samachar news agency reported.

B

Dr. Barnard Urges Active Euthanasia

WASHINGTON, April 27 (AP) — Dr. Christiaan Barnard, the South African surgeon who pioneered heart transplant operations, said yesterday that the time has come for doctors to practice active euthanasia to put hopeless and suffering patients out of misery.

Merely withdrawing modern life-support systems and halting efforts to save the dying is not sufficient in some cases, Dr. Barnard said in a panel discussion here.

C

Salvador Policeman Is Killed on Campus

SAN SALVADOR, Sept. 19 (AP) — Three young women armed with rifles killed a policeman patrolling the University of El Salvador campus yesterday and wounded another, authorities reported.

They said that the women, believed to be members of a leftist guerrilla gang, escaped. The Faribundo Marti Popular Liberation Force claimed responsibility for the attack, saying that it was retaliation for university police actions against a student demonstration Friday.

D

Suzie's voyage

SUZIE WONG, the killer whale from Clacton, arrived safely in Hong Kong over the weekend. Four-year-old Suzie was sold to Hong Kong for £110.000 after a storm destroyed her dolphinarium earlier this month. She was left wallowing in shallow water for about three hours before she could be rescued.—Reuter.

E

Suicide toll

MORE SWEDES died of suicide than in traffic accidents in 1978.. The suicide rate rose by 4 per cent last year, the Central Bureau of Statistics said yesterday. The bureau said 1,626 people died of suicide, while 1,073 deaths were caused by road accidents. — UPI.

F

Record rains take 1,291 lives in India

Delhi, Sept 27.—The Indian Government reported today that 1,291 lives had been lost, 26,687 head of cattle drowned, a million and a half dwellings damaged or destroyed and almost 43 million people displaced in the unprecedented rains that began in late June.

G

US satellite breaks up after 13 years

From Our Own Correspondent
Washington, Sept 17

Pegasus 1, an American research satellite launched 13 years ago, broke up over northern Angola early today as it reentered the Earth's atmosphere.

A spokesman for the National Aeronautics and Space Administration (Nasa) later told reporters that there had been no reports so far of anyone sighting burning parts of the space vehicle as it disintegrated.

The 23,000lb satellite was launched from Cape Kennedy in 1965 to study the distribution of space dust, or micrometeorites, near the Earth's surface. Its mission was completed when its radio transmitter was turned off in 1968 and it has since been orbiting the Earth aimlessly.

Nasa scientists who were tracking it said they expected any pieces which fell to Earth to be scattered over a corridor 125 miles wide and nearly 3,000 miles long. They said the likelihood of any debris causing damage was infinitesimal.

Colorado Springs: A spokesman for the National Air Defence Command said there was no apparent link between Pegasus 1 and reports of unidentified flying objects over New Mexico.—Reuter.

H

Naples 'Blood' Duly Liquefies

NAPLES, Sept. 19 (UPI) — The dark crystallized substance that Neapolitans believe to be the blood of St. Januarius liquefied on schedule today. The 8,000 persons in the church burst into applause, bells rang and people in the square outside set off firecrackers.

The thrice annual "miracle of St. Januarius" is awaited as an omen of what Heaven has in store for the city. The liquefaction is supposed to occur three times a year: on the Saturday before the first Sunday in May, on Sept. 19 and on Dec. 16.

According to tradition, Januarius was a bishop beheaded by Roman soldiers in the year 305, and the blood was collected by a pious woman after his death. The "miracle" has been recorded over the past 500 years, but there is no mention of it before the 14th century. Theories attribute it to the collective willpower of believers, volcanic activity at Mt. Vesuvius, exposure of the "blood" to light, or crass fraud.

I

Russians Tell How to Grow More Wheat

MOSCOW, Oct. 12 (AP) — The fields may soon be alive with the sound of music now that Soviet scientists have discovered they can improve their wheat crop by playing a 10-minute high-frequency concert for it.

Tass reported that experiments under way at Leningrad's Nikolai Vavilov plant-breeding institute have already demonstrated that the music can promote frost resistance, increase yield by as much as three times, and stimulate more-rapid germination.

Professor Vladimir Dorofeyev, head of the wheat department of the institute, said the high-frequency sound waves are one way of insuring healthy wheat in extreme circumstances.

J

Polar heatwave

While Europe and the United States have been shivering through an abnormally chilly spring, American scientists at the South Pole have reported the hottest April on record. 'Hot' for them means an average temperature of −50.6 C. The highest temperature of the month was −36.5 C, recorded on 24 April.

K Box Spills Kidnappers' Ransoms

ALESSANDRIA, Italy, Dec. 23 (AP.)—A box sent from a Sardinian worker in Milan to his wife back home turned out to be more than a Christmas present.

The box broke during transfer from one train to another in this north Italian town today and out spilled a surprise —180 million lire ($234,000) which the police said was ransom money from three separate kidnappings.

The police reported that quick checks with the police computer in Rome proved that the money was part of ransoms paid for the release of Genoa industrialist, Paolo Costa, the Milan confectionery maker Paolo Larraroni, and the Verona magnate Saverio Garonzi.

L Fare dodger shot

AN ELDERLY man, who jumped over an Underground railway turnstile in New York, to avoid paying a 50-cent fare, was shot to death by a transport policeman when he pulled a knife. — UPI.

---

4 Divide into groups with between three and five people in each. Each group is now the team of reporters responsible for producing an evening radio news programme. This programme consists of news headlines, followed by more detailed accounts of some of the news events. The programme usually describes five events and includes two or three interviews. You have already read the news content for this evening (see articles above). Your job now is to convert it into a short lively programme.

Section B

1 Your objective in this exercise is to scan the articles quickly for certain information. At this stage do not worry about detail that is not directly related to the information you are looking for. Do not attempt to understand each article completely. There are five articles. Before beginning to read article A, read the first question for that article. Quickly scan the article and underline the word, phrase, or sentence which answers the question. Repeat for all the questions. ⇒ page 99–B.

ARTICLE A
a) How many nations had to ratify the convention for it to become effective?
b) Which country originally made the proposal for the treaty?

UNITED NATIONS, N.Y., Oct. 12 (AP)—The United Nations announced yesterday that an international treaty against weather warfare had gone into effect.

The Legal Office said the convention on the prohibition of military or any other hostile use of environmental modification techniques entered into force when Laos ratified it last week.

The convention, which required ratification by 20 nations to become effective, aims to outlaw the employment in war of such practices as rainmaking, setting off earthquakes or starting tidal waves. The United States has not yet ratified it.

Environmental modification techniques are defined as any method of changing—through the deliberate manipulation of natural processes—the dynamics, composition or structure of the earth, including living things, rocks, water and air, or of outer space.

The treaty originated as a Soviet proposal and was approved by the General Assembly in December, 1976.

Besides Laos, the countries that have ratified it are Britain, Spain, Denmark, Finland, Cyprus, Tunisia, Ghana, Yemen, Sri Lanka, Mongolia, the Soviet Union, Belorussia, the Ukraine, Poland, East Germany, Czechoslovakia, Hungary, Bulgaria and Cuba.

a) On what condition will the world be declared free of smallpox?

b) Which techniques did the World Health Organisation use in its African campaign to eradicate smallpox?

c) What were the difficulties faced by the campaign in Ethiopia?

d) Why did campaign workers show villagers pictures of people who had smallpox?

From Victoria Brittain
in Nairobi

Only 10 years ago one million people died in a year from smallpox and millions more were scarred for life. But the World Health Organisation now believes that the disease has been conquered even in its last stronghold — the Horn of Africa.

The last recorded case in the world was in Merka Town, Somalia, on October 26, 1977. The world will be declared free of the disease in October next year if no new cases are discovered before then.

After a three-day meeting in Nairobi of doctors who have been dealing with smallpox, WHO is to be asked to consider offering a reward of several thousand dollars to anyone reporting a case of smallpox anywhere in the world.

Twenty African countries were selected for the campaign to eradicate smallpox by WHO in 1967. Instead of mass vaccination, the outbreaks were isolated by vaccinating in a ring round the affected village. So successful was the technique that the last cases were seen in West and Central Africa in 1970 and 1971.

East Africa has been less successful, partly because Ethiopia was a slow starter in the programme, according to Dr Isao Aritan of the WHO. The main difficulty, he says, is the nomads constantly on the move in Ethiopia and Somalia.

Well over 2,000 locally-trained volunteers have been used in Ethiopia and Somalia to conduct house-to-house or village-to-village searches with simple pictures of smallpox victims so that even the most isolated people know what the disease looks like. They have helped in the eradication by reporting cases for the reward, which is worth about £15.

from *The Guardian*

stronghold: centre

a) How often does the baby seal hunt take place?

b) Why were 12 demonstrators arrested?

c) How did the police release the protestors who chained themselves to the ships?

d) How did the demonstrators who dived into the sea get back to land?

By STUART GREIG

A VIOLENT battle erupted yesterday as an attempt was made to sabotage the annual killings of Canada's baby seals.

Twelve demonstrators were arrested when they tried desperately to stop the ships carrying the hunters leaving Newfoundland for the ice floes.

Fighting broke out as an angry crowd attacked the conservationists from the Greenpeace Movement.

Three of the protestors chained themselves to ships. Police smashed the padlocks with hammers.

Two other protesters dived into the freezing water to swim in the path of the vessels. They were picked up by coastguards.

The sabotage bid failed. All five ships left harbour for the cull, which begins on Saturday.

from *Daily Mirror*

cull: kill

ARTICLE D

a) Who is Mr David Simpson?
b) How are human rights violated in western Europe?
c) Who has been under house arrest for 13 years?

HUMAN RIGHTS were abused in at least 110 countries last year, according to the 1978 report of Amnesty International—"dismal reading" on the thirtieth anniversary of the Universal Declaration of Human Rights said Mr David Simpson, director of Amnesty's British section.

Announcing publication of the report yesterday, Mr Simpson said: "Prisoners of conscience are being held in at least 70 countries and we are investigating possible cases in a further 12 countries. Almost all of them are members of the United Nations."

The report maintains that kidnapping, torture, and killing have remained the systematic method of combating opposition in several Latin American and African countries. In Asia political dissidents were still held without trial. In Eastern Europe dissidents were stigmatised with "mental illness," and in Western Europe harsh laws against terrorism posed a potential threat to human rights.

Mr Martin Ennals, the secretary-general of Amnesty International, pointed to the increased length of the report over previous editions (321 pages), and said: "The lip service paid to human rights by governments has equally grown. This does not make our task easier. It means it is legitimate to talk about human rights but it does not mean it is legitimate to do anything about human rights."

While refusing to draw any "league table" of different countries, Amnesty notes that in Argentina 15,000 people disappeared in two years; in Indonesia there were 55,000 political prisoners in October 1977; in Algeria the former President, Mr Ahmed Ben Bella, last year "celebrated" his thirteenth year of house arrest.

Although the organisation commends amnesties in various parts of the world the report leaves almost no country unscathed by its criticism. Out of 4,726 "prisoners of conscience" adopted by Amnesty, 15 were in the United States.

from *The Guardian*

Amnesty International: an organisation which seeks the release of political prisoners

lip service: support which is stated verbally but not carried out

ARTICLE E

a) What is threatened by the increasing amount of theft in American hotels?
b) Does the American hotel industry lose more as a result of unpaid bills, or theft?
c) Who is Mr Kanner?
d) How does Mr Kanner explain that in 95% of the thefts, there is no sign of forced entry?

ALEXANDRIA, Va., Nov. 5—The hotel manager puts in a very busy and vexing morning. Thieves make off with a $2,000 statue from the lobby and a guest reports a stolen imported car. Then, late in the day, while the manager is still in a state of shock, the thieves come back and steal a piano.

This is not the plot for a new TV series about the pitfalls of running a hotel. It is a true story, illustrating an area of crime that has received little attention and which threatens the very existence of small hotel and motel operations in the United States, according to Merritt Kanner, senior vice president of Rocky Pomerance Associates, a Miami-based security consulting agency.

Speaking to the National Crime Prevention Association during a three-day conference that closed Friday, Mr. Kanner said most people think of crime in hotels and motels as no more than guests making off with souvenir towels, glasses and ashtrays. One guest in three will take something, he said, feeling that "taking is not stealing."

But that is the least of the problem. Some guests carry out furniture, tear off wallpaper and rip off pictures that are bolted to the walls. And besides the guests, there are the criminals who descend on motels and hotels bent on stealing or otherwise defrauding the establishment.

Overall, Mr. Kanner said, the industry loses $1 billion a year from theft, with another $30 million in losses from unpaid bills and bills paid with stolen credit cards and traveler's checks.

Mr. Kanner said that of all hotel-room thefts, 50 percent occur in unattended rooms, and in 95 percent of these cases, there is no sign of forced entry. He said one cause may be the 40,000 to 50,000 unreturned hotel keys that are in circulation at any one time.

from *International Herald Tribune*

20

2   You now have some facts from each of the articles in exercise 1. Your aim in this
    exercise is to find the central idea of each article.   ⇒ 100–C.   Read article A as
    quickly as possible. Answer the question about article A below. Repeat for all the
    articles.

The central idea of article A is:
i)   The United States has ratified the convention against weather warfare.
ii)   Last week Laos ratified the convention against weather warfare.
iii) The convention outlaws the employment in war of practices such as rainmaking,
      setting off earthquakes or starting tidal waves.
iv)   An international treaty against weather warfare has gone into effect.

The central idea of article B is:
i)   The last recorded case of smallpox in the world was in Somalia on 26 October
      1977.
ii)   The World Health Organisation believes that smallpox has been eradicated.
iii) Only ten years ago a million people died of smallpox.
iv)   In 1967 the World Health Organisation selected 20 African countries for the
      campaign to eradicate smallpox.

The central idea of article C is:
i)   After fighting broke out, demonstrators failed to sabotage the annual killing of
      baby seals in Canada.
ii)   The Greenpeace Movement is a conservationist group.
iii) Two demonstrators jumped into the freezing sea to stop the hunters leaving
      Newfoundland.
iv)   Police arrested 12 demonstrators in Newfoundland yesterday.

The central idea of article D is:
i)   The 1978 report of Amnesty International says that human rights were abused in
      at least 110 countries.
ii)   The Director of Amnesty's British section thought that the 1978 Amnesty report
      was dismal.
iii) The 1978 Amnesty report was longer than ever before.
iv)   The 1978 Amnesty report stated that prisoners of conscience are being held in at
      least 70 countries.

The central idea of article E is:
i)   American hotel managers have a very difficult job.
ii)   Crime in American hotels and motels has become a serious and costly problem.
iii) The majority of guests at American hotels steal souvenir towels, glasses or
      ashtrays.
iv)   A new TV series will deal with the problems and difficulties involved in running
      a hotel.

3   Write headlines for each of the articles you have just read. Try to make your
    headlines as dramatic and as condensed as possible and make sure that they convey
    the central idea of the articles they accompany.

Section C

1   Scan the article 'Inmate-cowboys begin competition at prison rodeo' in order to answer the following questions. Work as quickly as possible. Do not worry about detail that is not directly related to the information you are looking for.   ⇒ page 99–B.
    a) Where did the rodeo take place?
    b) What happens at a rodeo?
    c) How many different kinds of spectator were there at the rodeo? Name them.
    d) How long does this rodeo usually last?
    e) What was the weather like on the first Sunday of the rodeo?
    f) Who is Willie Craig?
    g) How well did Willie Craig do in last year's rodeo?

2   Read the article again more carefully. On page 23 are seven words and expressions taken from the article. In each case decide which of the four alternatives following the word or expression is most similar in meaning to it in the context of the article. ⇒ page 100–D.

Inmate-cowboys begin competition at prison rodeo

By FRANK KRYSTYNIAK
Post Correspondent

HUNTSVILLE — The Texas Prison Rodeo is a one-of-a-kind event — the wildest of men thrown into the same arena with the wildest of animals — with thousands of spectators urging them on.

The spectator mix is a curious one — as curious perhaps as the event itself. All types were there Sunday as the rodeo opened for its 47th Annual October of mayhem.

There were spectators who are obviously real cowboys, and there are still a few of those in Texas, who came simply to see the rodeo. They wore faded jeans, well-broken-in boots, and sweaty straw hats.

THERE WERE THE newcomers to Southeast Texas. They came as a sort of initiation rite, so they too could shake their heads at the office Monday and marvel at the whole spectacle. They were dressed in sport shirts and ties and their little girls wore pink birthday party dresses.

There were a few whose western clothes were too new and whose skin was too white. The prison guards knew them and pointed them out and said that they had been inmates only a short time ago.

But most of the opening Sunday crowd were the repeat visitors, the average, everyday folks who come back every year. Maybe not every year, but when times get hard and their lives start to drag, they can come back to the shadows of the red brick walls, look at the white sea of inmate spectators, and remind themselves that things could be worse.

Even the 15-minute traffic jam in Huntsville every Sunday afternoon in October must seem like the Indianapolis Speedway in comparison to every afternoon on the Katy Freeway.

IT WAS AN AVERAGE opening Sunday crowd of 7,000, and even a bit better than the first Sunday last year. The 1977 five-Sunday attendance totaled 96,000, and the event raised $300,000 for special medical, recreational and other small luxury items not appropriated by the Legislature.

A few of those attending Sunday came to hear special entertainment by The Kendalls, a father-daughter team with only one "big hit" to date, *Heaven's Just a Sin Away*. Guest stars for subsequent Sundays will be Larry Gatlin Oct. 8, Tom T. Hall Oct. 15, Tammy Wynette Oct. 22, and Freddy Fender Oct. 29.

The big stars Sunday, however, were the inmates, who took a "there's-no-tomorrow" approach to each event. The more dangerous the event, the more they seemed to like it.

There was 58-year-old Willie Craig, the greying native of Greensville who is doing a 30-year sentence at the Ellis Unit.

CRAIG FINISHED A disappointing sixth in the overall standings last year after leading through the mid-point in the competition. As the weather got cooler last fall and his bad knee got stiffer, Willie became less sure that he would be around this year to compete for that elusive all-around title.

The knee is better, however, and so are Willie's spirits. He was up to his old crowd-pleasing tricks again in the high-80 degree weather of Sunday's opener. He finished first in Bareback Bronc Riding and third in Saddle Bronc Riding.

from *The Houston Post*

mayhem: violent destruction or confusion
big hit: popular success

a) *one of a kind*
   i)   ordinary
   ii) not like others
   iii) cruel
   iv) exciting

b) *urging them on*
   i)   encouraging them
   ii) throwing things at them
   iii) running after them
   iv) watching them

c) *faded*
   i)   losing colour
   ii) tight-fitting
   iii) dirty
   iv) old

d) *sweaty*
   i)   out of shape
   ii) 'wet from perspiration
   iii) home-made
   iv) yellow

e) *initiation rite*
   i)   punishment
   ii) duty
   iii) attempt to ride
   iv) admittance procedure

f) *inmates*
   i)   friends of the prison guards
   ii) visitors to the prison
   iii) ex–prisoners
   iv) prisoners

g) *drag*
   i)   pass slowly
   ii) pass quickly
   iii) be full of problems
   iv) be dangerous

4

BUSINESS NEWS ▬▬▬▬

Section A

1   Your aim in this exercise is to find the central idea of each article.   ⇒ page 100–C.
Read article A as quickly as you can without losing the sense of what you are
reading. Answer the question about article A below and then go on immediately to
the next article. Repeat for all the articles.

ARTICLE A

THE BATTLE over food prices moves into a new war zone this week. Key Markets, the supermarket subsidiary of food group Fitch Lovell, is jumping on to a promotional bandwagon which has retained the affections of American shoppers since 1963 : the shopping game.

Tomorrow, 1.6 to 2 million Key Market Cash Bingo cards will be distributed to households near its 124 stores. This will be followed by a seven-day television campaign, to start on Wednesday. By Thursday, the first shoppers could be scanning the boards in the local Key Market to see whether their lucky number is being flashed to an expectant world.

Key Markets' game is a variant of bingo, and the ground rules will be familiar

to all devotees of that pastime. The cards distributed will carry a number which could correspond with one of the seven numbers displayed each week in Key Market branches.

If it does : Bingo ! Shoppers will be in line for 50p, £1, £5, £10, £100, £1,000 or £5,000 prizes. Some 150,0000 prizes in all, worth £450,000, will be distributed over the

12 weeks in which the first game will run. Cash bingo tickets will also be distributed to adults passing through a Key Market check-out during this period.

Key Markets is hoping to emulate the success of American supermarkets. Americans estimate that shopping games increase store traffic by 15 to 20 per cent, and that this traffic sticks when stores also offer competitive goods and prices.

Key Markets says its new venture will not affect its prices, as prize money will come out of normal promotional expenditure. And if its game hits no legal snags (Key Markets has counsel's opinion that it does not contravene gaming and lottery regulations), there is little doubt that other supermarket giants will be ready to follow suit.

from *The Observer*

jumping onto a bandwagon: following the latest idea because it is fashionable
bingo: a gambling game like lotto played with cards divided into numbered squares
be in line for: likely to get

The central idea of article A is:
i)   Shopping games increase traffic in American supermarkets by 15 to 20%.
ii)   The shopping game will slightly increase prices at Key Market stores.
iii) Key Markets is going to introduce a version of the American shopping game to its stores in Britain.
iv)   Because the shopping is like Bingo, participants will easily learn the rules.

WASHINGTON—Prices for basic necessities — food, shelter, energy and health care—rose last year at nearly double the rate of all other items, the National Center for Economic Alternatives said.

The center, a liberal research group that monitors inflation among necessities, said these prices rose an average of 10.8% in 1978, compared with a rise of 6.4% for all other items. In 1977, prices of necessities rose 8.3% and non-necessities 4.8%.

The research group said 70% of the budgets of four out of five Americans goes to buy necessities, and it has been urging the Carter administration to concentrate its anti-inflation efforts on these items.

from *The Wall Street Journal*

The central idea of article B is:

i) The cost of basic necessities rose last year at nearly twice the rate of all other items.

ii) The major part of the incomes of most Americans is spent on necessities.

iii) The National Center for Economic Alternatives has defined basic necessities as being food, shelter, energy, and health care.

iv) The price of necessities rose an average of 10.8% in 1978.

ROBOTS designed and made in Japan by Fujitsu Fanuc are to be marketed by Hydro Machine Tools, of Halstead, Essex (a member of the 600 Group), in the UK at prices ranging from £25,000 to £60,000.

Basically, the machines are programmed pick-and-place mechanical arms and hands, and will complement the company's existing numerically controlled lathes, making it possible to produce turned components without human attention.

One of the units, Sirobot 2, has five basic movements and can move bodily up and down, rotate on its own axis, move backwards and forwards horizontally, while the picking hand is able to twist or tilt.

As a result, the robot can supply five associated metal removal machines placed around it with stock metal and remove the finished components to off-loading stations.

Introducing the new units, 600 Group chairman Sir Jack Wellings said that although considerable initial effort will be needed in the UK to make such systems acceptable, their ultimate use was "absolutely inevitable" and the company was determined to be in at the early stages of growth.

There are probably under 100 such installations in the UK at the moment, compared with an estimated 20,000 to 25,000 in Japan—a figure described by Sir Jack as "frightening."

from *Financial Times*

The central idea of article C is:

i) Robots are used in Japan more than in Britain.

ii) A British firm is going to market robots designed and made in Japan.

iii) British workers will not accept robots.

iv) Robots have five basic movements.

ARTICLE D

Special to THE WALL STREET JOURNAL

ENGELSKIRCHEN, West Germany —More than 100 years after Karl Marx wrote "Das Kapital," the business that financed it is folding.

Hermann Engels, the 46-year-old great grandson of the younger brother of Friedrich Engels, announced that he had sold the family textile factory, Ermen & Engels, to a realty concern and that it will be razed along with the 48-room family mansion, the Braunswerth Palace, to make room for a housing project.

Friedrich Engels, the friend and collaborator of Marx, used his income from the family business to support Marx and his family while Marx worked on the books that laid the groundwork for socialism and communism.

Friedrich Engels scorned the business, saying "it's bad enough to be a bourgeois without being a manufacturer too." But he took the income.

The German textile business has been hard hit by competition from Asia, and Hermann Engels said the company has been losing money for years. Its staff has dropped from 250 in 1960 to the present 35.

from *The Wall Street Journal*

folding : closing, collapsing
razed : completely demolished

The central idea of article D is:

i)   Engels financed Marx while the latter was writing *Das Kapital*.

ii) The business that financed *Das Kapital* has recently been losing a lot of money.

iii) The business that financed *Das Kapital* has been sold.

iv) Hermann Engels has sold the family business because he doesn't like being a bourgeois manufacturer.

ARTICLE E

Ross Mark in Washington

A COMPUTER designed to ferret out mistakes in the U.S. Government payroll, approved a payment of £45,000 to Donald Duck.

It also sent out similar cheques to Mr Mickey Mouse, his wife Minnie, and 27 other cartoon characters, in a test set by investigators.

The blunders of the "foolproof" computer were uncovered during investigations into Washington's latest scandal involving a £3,500,000 pay fraud.

The money was paid as overtime to 600 Government employees — most of them working in the Justice Department—using fictitious names.

In some cases the names used were those of employees who had resigned years ago.

Mr H. L. Kreiger, the chief investigator, said, "That computer should have rejected the payment to Donald Duck on two grounds : First he wasn't on the payroll, and secondly, the maximum federal salary is half that paid out to the cartoon character. "There is evidence of an elaborate swindle."

from *Daily Express*

ferret out : search for
swindle : fraud

The central idea of article E is:

i)   Donald Duck is on the US government payroll.

ii) During an investigation into a US government pay fraud, payments were made to 29 cartoon characters.

iii) Cartoon characters earn a lot of money.

iv) The employees of the Justice Department in Washington are dishonest.

2 Below you will find the headlines for the above articles. Match the headlines and the articles. ⇒ page 99–A. Do you think that any of the headlines convey the central idea of the article particularly well?

1 *Prices of Necessities Up*
At Double Others' Pace

2 ## No need for the human hand

3 # DONALD DUCK SWINDLE

4 ## Bingo! in the shops

5 *Business That Financed*
'Das Kapital' Is Folding

3 Scan the articles again in order to answer the following questions. Work as quickly as possible. Do not worry about detail that is not directly related to the information you are looking for. ⇒ page 99–B.

ARTICLE A
a) How long has the shopping game been in operation in America?
b) How many Key Market stores are there?
c) How long will the television advertising campaign last?
d) Do shoppers have to pay for their Cash Bingo cards?
e) How do shoppers know if they have won?
f) How much is the biggest prize worth?
g) How long will the first game run?
h) Where will the prize money come from?

ARTICLE B
a) What is the National Center for Economic Alternatives?
b) By how much did the cost of non-necessities rise in 1977?
c) What percentage of most Americans' budgets goes on necessities?

ARTICLE C
a) Who designed the robots described in the article?
b) What do the robots consist of?
c) In which directions can the robots move? Draw a diagram showing the different movements.
d) Why is Sir Jack Wellings introducing the robots?

ARTICLE D
a) How is Hermann Engels related to Friedrich Engels?
b) What kind of factory has Engels sold?
c) What is the Braunswerth Palace?
d) What will be built in place of the factory?
e) How many people were employed in the factory in 1960?

ARTICLE E
a) What was the purpose of the computer described in the article?
b) How many cartoon characters received cheques?
c) How many employees received part of the £3,500,000?
d) Why should the computer not have authorised payment to Donald Duck?

Section B

1   Scan the article 'Life when panic is over' in order to answer the following questions. Work as quickly as possible. Do not worry about detail that is not directly related to the information you are looking for. ⇒ page 99–B.
a) How old is Diana McLaughlin?
b) How many American marriages end in divorce?
c) What is Cruse?
d) How many sessions are there in 'Sorting it out'?
e) What do the women learn to do in the final part of the course?
f) What is Magic Mop?

2   Below you will find statements about the information contained in the article you have just read. Decide whether the statements are true or false. If a statement is false, correct it. You will need to read the article in more detail to do this exercise.
a) Diana McLaughlin was in her thirties when she got a divorce.
b) The Maryland Centre depends on private donations.
c) Congress has set up centres similar to the Maryland Centre in all 50 states of the USA.
d) The Maryland Centre aims to help widowed, divorced and separated women who suddenly face life on their own.
e) Lani Lovern was helped by the Maryland Centre.

28

3 Divide into small groups and discuss the following questions. Be prepared to report back to the whole class giving reasons for your opinions and conclusions.

a) '(The Centre) ... provides facilities for women over 35 who face financial disaster through bereavement, separation or divorce and are unlikely to find employment because they were primarily homemakers.' The women described in the article live in the USA. Does this situation also exist in your own country? Do you think that an organisation like the Maryland Centre would be useful/necessary in your country?

b) Do you think that women should stay at home to care for their children?

c) Do you think that men should stay at home to care for their children?

d) The Maryland Centre is financed by the state. Do you agree that this kind of organisation should be paid for with tax-payers' money?

Life when panic is over

DIANA McLaughlin arrived at Baltimore airport with two suitcases and a dollar in her pocket: only that after 34 years as a wife to a merchant marine officer and caring for four children.

At 56, recently divorced, she had no idea how to find employment. Two years later, she holds down a responsible job helping women to start successful businesses.

Diana's salvation was worked by the Maryland Centre for Displaced Homemakers, which helped 1,400 American women last year. Its facilities, paid for by state grant, are available to women over 35 (younger women are thought capable of fending for themselves) who face financial disaster through bereavement, separation or divorce and are unlikely to find employment because they were primarily homemakers. The problem is so immense—one in three American marriages end in divorce and three million widows are created a year—that there have been moves in Congress to set up similar centres in all 50 states of the U S A.

In Britain there are no such facilities. The DHSS wards off starvation with supplementary benefit and the Citizens' Advice Bureau provides telephone numbers of groups like Cruse which counsel and guide grief. But there are no courses to rehabilitate the widow or divorcee.

This is just what the Maryland Centre aims to do. Of the women it salvaged in its first year, at a cost of about £800 a head, nearly two-thirds are now working.

Six sessions called Sorting It Out aim to "increase every woman's potential in what she wants to do." She is encouraged to assess her income requirements, the areas of employment open to her, and coaxed to acquire more skills through the centre's courses.

Next comes Time and Stress Management, designed to reduce self-sacrifice to relations and children. The women are taught to allocate their time carefully, putting some aside for job-hunting and planning their daily routine.

In the final part of the course they learn to recognise their talents. If they have made out shopping lists, they could compile inventories for a store; if they have arranged church bazaars, they have telephone experience and organising skills; if they have drawn up rotas for fetching the children from school, they could design work schedules.

For those still unsure of themselves, sheltered employment is provided by internships of 26 weeks in a friendly environment, combined with supportive workshops at the centre. Capital is even lent to start small businesses, the most successful of which is Magic Mop, an independent cleaning contractors consisting of four women. Its organiser, Lani Lovern, made £6,000 last year, working only four days a week.

Cynthia Hall

DHSS: Department of Health and Social Security
supplementary benefit: payment made by government to people in need e.g. unemployed
bazaar: sale of goods for charity

Section C

1　Look at the article 'Chips are down for jobs' which follows. Before beginning to read the article, read question (a) carefully. Quickly scan the article for the answer. Underline the word, phrase or sentence which answers the question. Repeat for all the questions. Do not worry about detail that is not directly related to the meaning to it in the context of the article.　⇒ page 100–D.

   a) What are silicon chips?
   b) What kind of worries were fashionable before the silicon chip revolution?
   c) Who discussed the problem of the effect of the microprocessor on employment, in Nice last week?
   d) How many occupations could, in theory, be replaced by microprocessors?
   e) What does Dr George Champine think will happen?
   f) What does Carolyn Hayman think will happen?
   g) What trivial thing can microprocessors already do?
   h) What will happen to the British economy if it does not accept and use microprocessors?

2　Divide into groups with three or four people in each and discuss the following questions. Be prepared to report back to the whole class giving reasons for your opinions and conclusions.

   a) In which fields and for what purposes are microprocessors already being used?
   b) In which fields and for what purposes do you think they will be used in the future?
   c) In what ways could microprocessors change our everyday life?
   d) It has been said that the transistor was the first revolution in electronics, and the microprocessor is the second. Do you agree with this statement? Why? Why not?

Chips are down for jobs

from NIGEL HAWKES, our Science Correspondent in Nice

ARE FIVE million jobs in Britain about to be replaced by tiny chips of silicon? It is a prospect that is sending shivers down the spines of Ministers, civil servants, academics and trade union leaders.

The silicon chips are, of course, microprocessors, minute but highly sophisticated electronic circuits suited to an almost infinite variety of applications, from the humble pocket calculator to the control of entire automated factories and warehouses.

The effects the microprocessor will have on employment are the subject of intense argument. For those who like to keep their worries in fashion, the silicon chip revolution has taken over from pollution, the energy crisis and the bomb as a subject of concern.

For three days last week a small group which included Government, political, trade union, industry and press representatives discussed the problem at the Sperry Univac Executive Centre at Saint-Paul-de-Vence, near Nice.

Almost everybody agreed there was a problem. The list of jobs that could in theory be replaced by microprocessors is long and alarming.

A report prepared for the Computer, Systems and Electronics Requirements Board, but still unpublished, lists 29 occupations at risk, starting with proof readers and including postmen, draughts-men, secretaries, filing clerks, meter readers, plateprinters, assembly workers, warehousemen, sales clerks and many others.

But the real issue is not whether jobs will be lost in some sectors of the economy —that is a normal effect of advancing technology — but whether they will be replaced by other jobs in the new industries the microprocessor will replace. There the arguments begin.

The American and Japanese view is that concern over the issue has been exaggerated. Dr George Champine, director of Advanced Systems for Sperry Univac in the United States, claimed that 'literally thousands' of new products would emerge from the microprocessor re-

30

volution.

'Every time technology advances people forecast unemployment. The mechanical reaper, the cotton gin, and the first computers 30 years ago were all supposed to cause massive unemployment,' Dr Champine said. 'But it didn't happen.'

Miss Carolyn Hayman, a young economist from the Central Policy Review Staff— the Government's 'Think Tank'—also took a relatively optimistic view. She thought it likely that the service industries could continue to absorb people displaced

The gloomy viewpoint was put by Dr Ray Curnow, of the First Policy Research Unit at Sussex University, who said that Britain needs to find new jobs at a staggering rate, equal to 6 per cent a year, just to stay where it is.

'It will be economic to use the microprocessor to do the most trivial things,' he said.

One of the trivial things microprocessors can already do is to dispense cocktails. At the press of a button the 'electronic bartender' will deliver a perfect Bloody Mary or a Martini mixed to individual taste. Participants at the seminar were stirred rather than shaken by this news.

The Japanese Government has switched its emphasis away from heavy industries like shipbuilding and steel making and towards microprocessor-based products.

So the option of going slowly in Britain seems to be closed, unless we retreat into a siege economy and ban imports. Either we embrace the microprocessor and lose jobs through displacement or we reject it and lose jobs through a catastrophic loss of international competitiveness. It is a challenging and alarming choice.

from *The Observer*

chips are down: the time has come to face the problem

Section D

1   Look at the following article 'Management tools'. Before beginning to read the article, read question (a) below carefully. Quickly scan the article for the answer. Underline the word, phrase or sentence which answers the question. Repeat for all the questions. Do not worry about detail that is not directly related to the information you are looking for.   ⇒ page 99–B.
   a)   What is 'Protection Management'?
   b)   What do the mannequins in department stores often have in their eyes?
   c)   Who are the unemployed actors employed by?
   d)   Who is Anthony Reichet?
   e)   What is the truth test replacing?
   f)   What was published in the *Journal of Applied Psychology*?
   g)   How fast can Sentry II travel?

Management Tools

In battling the growing problem of employee theft, business is in no mood to scoff at any stratagem. Some of the latest:

● "Rent-A-Thief," according to the newsletter "Protection Management," operates on the premise that theft can be reduced by setting a thief to catch a thief. The service hires out unemployed actors who take jobs in companies and begin stealing as prearranged, letting other employees know what's going on. Suddenly, and with great uproar, the thief is caught, given a chewing out in sight of everyone, dismissed on the spot and dragged off screaming by security people — thus setting an example of the humiliation that awaits those who give in to a larcenous impulse.

● In department stores, mannequins often lead double lives. As they display the current fashions, their camera eyes transmit a TV image of the cash-register areas to watchers in a security room.

● Sentry II, a robot security guard, can be hired to work fulltime (no lunch breaks, no vacations, no weekends off, no holidays) from Quasar Industries, Rutherford, N.J. According to its inventor, Anthony Reichet, Sentry II, which stands about 6 feet tall, is able to "pursue an intruder at 48 miles an hour, issue verbal warnings.— (Re-
⟫⟫→

main still. Do not move. Under no conditions go near or touch any parts of my structure) — give off a blinding strobe light, shoot laugning gas and distinguish authorized from unauthorized personnel."

• The "truth test" is gaining as a substitute for the lie detector as a device to screen job applicants. One such test for which considerable validity is claimed — since it has achieved a hue of academic status through a research paper published in the Journal of Applied Psychology — is called the Reid Report. It consists of a series of questions for job applicants — the answers to which are designed to identify potential stealers.

from *The New York Times*

2 Below are six words and expressions taken from the article. In each case decide which of the four alternatives following the word or expression is most similar in meaning to it in the context of the article. ⇒ page 100–D.

a) *battling*
   i) considering
   ii) finishing
   iii) fighting
   iv) disliking

b) *scoff at*
   i) refuse
   ii) laugh at
   iii) pay for
   iv) take notice of

c) *uproar*
   i) planning
   ii) movement upwards
   iii) a lot of noise
   iv) speed

d) *chewing out*
   i) piece of chewing gum
   ii) interview
   iii) some advice
   iv) reprimand

e) *dragged off*
   i) searched
   ii) taken away unwillingly
   iii) undressed by force
   iv) knocked to the ground

f) *larcenous*
   i) bad
   ii) stupid
   iii) clever
   iv) stealing

3 Divide into groups with three or four people in each and discuss the following questions. Be prepared to report back to the whole class giving reasons for your opinions and conclusions.
   a) Is shoplifting common in your country?
   b) How are shops in your country protected against theft?
   c) In the article four novel ways of protecting shops against theft are described. Can you think of any others?
   d) Do you think that shoplifting is a serious offence? Why? Why not?
   e) How is shoplifting punished/dealt with in your country? How do you think it should be dealt with?

Section E

Writing narrative from cartoon strip. Put the pictures in the right order and then tell the story.

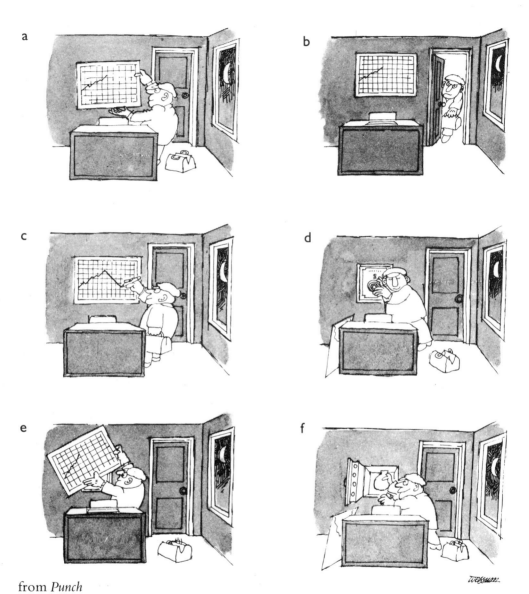

from *Punch*

5

TECHNOLOGY AND SCIENCE ▬

Section A

1   Each week the magazine *Newsweek* devotes a page to describing 'New Products and Processes'. Below you will find a selection of articles which have appeared on this page. Read the articles to find out the essential facts about each new invention.
⇒ page 99–B.   For each product or process, write down
a) who developed it;
b) where it was developed;
c) what kind of person/institution might benefit from it;
d) how much it costs;
e) in what kind of newspaper or magazine you think it should be advertised.

2   For each product or process, summarise its use in one sentence.

3   You work for an agency where you specialise in writing adverts for new inventions. Choose one of the inventions and write a newspaper or a television advert for it.

4   Each year a committee meets to decide which invention should be given the 'Award of the Year'. At the meeting each committee member briefly describes one of the products and then the relative merits of the inventions are discussed. This year *you* are the committee. Follow the procedure outlined, and decide in your groups which product should receive the 'Award of the Year'.

Lift-off

For about a year, some police cars in Brazil have been equipped with a kind of inflatable jack—an air bag that attaches to a vehicle's exhaust pipe and inflates with thousands of pounds of lifting force **(photo)**. Developed by Anser Electronica, Ltd., of São Paulo, the inflatable jack is now being introduced outside Latin America by Sturges Marketing Corp., of Westport, Conn.

As a replacement for conventional mechanical and hydraulic jacks, it is said to be safer, quicker and easier to use. The collapsed heavy-duty plastic bag is simply slipped under the car, its 7-foot-long hose is attached to the exhaust pipe and, when the engine is started, the bag inflates in less than a minute. Unlike other jacks, the Super Lift grips firmly on uneven terrain, such as snow, ice, sand or mud. Since it can be deflated and stored in a box no larger than an attaché case, the Super Lift is suitable for use by civilian motorists as well as highway emergency personnel. Price: $100, or $110 for a large-vehicle size.

Disappearing Ink

The Paper Mate Division of the Gillette Co., in Boston, Mass., has introduced a ballpoint pen with erasable ink. Called the Eraser Mate, it uses ink that has many of the same properties as rubber cement and, unless two days have passed, can be erased as easily as pencil markings. After that time, it becomes permanent. To accommodate the extremely thick ink (100 times thicker than ordinary ballpoint-pen ink), the manufacturer designed a pressurized cartridge that provides another advantage: the pen writes at any angle, even upside down. The pen comes with its own eraser and a replacement is included with refills. Price: $1.69; $1.19 for refills.

Voice of Conscience

Imagine if every time you went to the refrigerator or food cupboard, a voice scolded: "Are you eating again? No wonder you look the way you do. You'll be sorry, fatty." Chances are, you would cut down on those in-between-meal snacks so ruinous to your diet. That's the idea behind a new battery-powered device that acts as a constant reminder to dieters with little will-power. Called the Diet Conscience, the tiny gadget fits on practically any refrigerator or cabinet shelf and has a switch that activates it the moment the door is opened. Its eighteen-second recording is purposely offensive and will repeat itself indefinitely until the door is closed. According to its developer, Carol Kiebala of Leca, Ltd., in Palatine, Ill., the Diet Conscience can't stop you from sneaking leftovers or a second dessert—but it will certainly make you feel guilty when you do. Price: about $10.

Triple Telecast

For television fans who can't make up their minds about which station to watch, a Taiwanese manufacturer has come up with a solution. Sampo Corp., of Taipei, has introduced a three-screen television set **(photo).** The unit features a 19-inch color screen flanked on one side by a pair of 5-inch, black-and-white screens mounted one above the other. Three channels can be watched at once, and, using a remote control, a viewer can rotate simultaneous broadcasts from one screen to another simply by pressing a button. One or both of the smaller screens can also be hooked up to a closed-circuit camera, thus functioning as a security-surveillance monitor. Price: about $900.

Talking Scales

The American Foundation for the Blind, of New York, N.Y., is putting advanced technology to work for the handicapped. Using microprocessor-based voice circuits, engineers at the foundation have designed a collection of "talking" health aids. Two of these devices, a bathroom scale and a body-temperature thermometer, will be put on the market next spring. Both the scale and the thermometer include speakers and electronic equipment that enable them to call out the user's weight or temperature, while the scale also has a digital-display panel. Working with Detecto Scales, Inc., of Brooklyn, N.Y., the foundation has also produced an institutional-style floor scale for use in hospitals or nursing homes. Price: $1,000 for the Detecto institutional scale; about $100 for the home bathroom scale; about $150 for the thermometer.

Super Dropper

The capacity of ordinary kitchen teaspoons varies widely from one to another. So when a prescription for liquid medication calls for, say, 1 teaspoon, administering an accurate dosage at home is all but impossible. The problem is further complicated when the medicine must be dispensed in a fractional amount, by the cubic centimeter (cc) or in drops. Recently, Apex Medical Supply, Inc., of Bloomington, Minn., began marketing a precisely calibrated medicine dropper that can eliminate the danger of harmful misdosages in the home. The 5-inch-long Super Dropper has teaspoon and cc calibrations permanently etched on its plastic stem. The natural-rubber bulb on the dropper enables the user to draw and dispense an accurate amount of liquid medicine with no danger of spills, making the device especially useful when potent medicines must be given to children or infants. Price: about 79 cents.

Combating Spills at Sea

Last March, David Usher stood by helplessly as raging, 20-foot waves battered the grounded tanker Amoco Cadiz and spilled the ship's oil cargo into the ocean. More than 200,000 tons of oil ravaged marine wildlife and the shoreline of Brittany. To Usher, president of the oil-spill-control firm Marine Pollution Control, of Detroit, Mich., the scene was a replay of a spill two years earlier, when heavy seas prevented his crew from unloading the stricken Argo Merchant. That ship dumped tons of oil into the water off Nantucket, Mass. Determined to avoid such disasters in the future, Usher has developed a salvage-equipment package called HOS-E: Hazardous Off-Loading Systems-Emergencies.

Basically, HOS-E consists of portable work platforms that can be airlifted by helicopter and secured to the deck of a stricken tanker with heavy magnets and cables or large mechanical claws. The platforms can be leveled and stabilized even on listing ships by adjusting their hydraulic legs. Hoses and pumps can be positioned and operated by work crews on board the platforms, which also feature protective shelters large enough for three men. The pumping equipment also can be operated by remote control, with the robot arms on the platforms doing the work. Pumping operations can continue regardless of most weather conditions and thus—Usher is convinced—help prevent future ecological destruction.

Early-Warning System

Automobile manufacturers and electronics firms have spent millions of dollars trying to develop anti-collision radar for motor vehicles. Yet none of their results has proved economically feasible; in some cases, the radar would cost more than the car itself. Now a British manufacturer claims to have designed an inexpensive radar system based on a microwave technique adapted from missile-guidance technology.

Lawrence Electronics of Bradford, England, says the key to this low-cost system is a small transmitting and receiving device called a "waveguide," which is mounted on the front of a car and connected to a dashboard warning instrument. In circumstances such as dense fog or heavy rain, the radar would warn a driver of obstacles up to 300 feet ahead—whether they are stationary or moving. According to the manufacturer, the radar system could be offered as optional equipment for about the same price as a good-quality car radio.

Joggers' Pacesetter

Joggers who want to control their running speed can take advantage of a new pace-setting device designed by Majima Co., Ltd., of Tokyo, Japan. The wristwatch-style Running Pulse Master emits a steady 65-decibel beeping tone that helps a runner regulate his or her stride. An adjustable rhythm dial allows the user to vary the rate from 100 to 240 tones per minute. Powered by an ordinary 3-volt watch battery, the Running Pulse Master's vibrating-crystal sounding element is guaranteed for 1,000 hours of even-paced jogging. Price: $40.

from *Newsweek*

Section B

1   On pages 38–40 you will find six articles and the headlines which appeared with them. Match the articles and the headlines.   ⇒ page 99–A.

2   Scan the same articles for the information required in the questions below. Do not worry about detail that is not directly related to the information you are looking for. Do not attempt to understand each article completely.   ⇒ page 99–B.
   a)   When was the last major solar maximum?
   b)   What is Mr Sargent's job?
   c)   What can be seen on the last frame of the first UFO film?
   d)   What was Peter Suthert looking for when he studied the UFO films?
   e)   In which magazine did the article on heart attacks appear?
   f)   How wide is the ring around Jupiter?
   g)   What increase should be made in the EEC's budget for solar energy research, according to Mr Gretz?
   h)   Where is the recently discovered 'black hole'?
   i)   Why are 'black holes' invisible?

3   Decide whether the following statements are true or false, according to the information in the articles on pages 38–40. If a statement is false, correct it. You will need to read the articles in more detail to do this exercise.
   a)   The Voyager 1 spacecraft has entered the ring around Jupiter.
   b)   The recently discovered 'black hole' is 5,000,000,000 times the mass of the sun.
   c)   Dr Stuart Malin thinks that changes in the earth's magnetism are the cause of heart attacks.
   d)   By the year 2000 solar energy will provide 3% of the EEC's energy requirements.
   e)   Mr Sargent thinks that the next 11 years will be good ones for ham operators.
   f)   The two films showing supposed unidentified objects were both taken by businessmen.

37

1 Amazing link between magnetism and hearts

2 'Black hole' theory

3 Inconclusive case for UFO

4 Sunny side up for EEC

5 *New Sun Cycle Expected to Aid Ham, Citizen Band Radio Users*

6 *Voyager Finds Jupiter Ring*

A

SAN FRANCISCO, Dec. 9.—The sun is just entering a new 11-year cycle and, if it proves to be as active by 1980 as Howard Sargent 3d believes it will, it should affect ham radio operators, citizens band operators and satellite designers.

Mr. Sargent is the chief solar forecaster for the Space Environment Services Center, a part of the National Oceanic and Atmospheric Administration in Boulder, Colo. He made his forecast Wednesday at a meeting of the American Geophysical Union here. Mr. Sargent said that the 11 years ahead could be the second most active period for the sun in the last 100 years. If so, then it probably will affect high-frequency radio communication wavelengths, such as those used by hams and citizen band users, and perhaps satellites.

The radiation from the sun interacts with the earth's upper atmosphere. During the time of a so-called "maximum period" in the solar cycle, when sunspot activity and solar flares are more frequent, the disturbances on earth are much more pronounced.

"It will be good times for ham operators," Mr. Sargent said, "because radio propagation patterns are much better during times like that." Those with citizens band radios also will find their signals reaching a greater distance. But, Mr. Sargent said, this probably will glut the fixed citizen band channels with transmissions and citizen band users will be broadcasting into what, in effect, will be huge party lines.

As for satellites, Mr. Sargent said that a great many have been launched since the late 1950s, the time of the last major solar maximum, and designers may not have anticipated the intense solar radiation which the spacecraft might face. He said some satellites may be a little "more vulnerable to radiation damage than their builders had expected them to be."

ham: a licensed amateur radio operator

B

ALMOST everyone, it seems, has seen a UFO these days, but hard vidence to back up those claims is a rare treasure.

Last week, eight physicists and a Ministry of Defence representative gathered in a viewing theatre at Kodak's London headquarters to examine two amateur cine films showing supposed unidentified objects.

However, the meeting's conclusions served only to emphasise the view of sceptics that UFOs are misperceptions of the countless natural or man-made objects that fill our skies.

The first film, taken in January 1973 by a surveyor near Cuddington, Oxfordshire, shows a single luminous object moving out from behind some trees and travelling horizontally above the ground before suddenly vanishing. On the last frame of ⋙→

38

the film, trees are apparently bent over by some mysterious force as the UFO vanishes.

The second movie, taken by a businessman from Crewe, contains several sequences shot in October 1977 near Stonehenge. Luminous objects both singly and in formation, are seen apparently hovering in the darkening evening sky.

Both films have been widely shown on television, but this meeting, organised by the Committee for Scientific Investigation of Claims of the Paranormal, was the first time they had been subjected to close scientific scrutiny.

Peter Suthert, Kodak film analyst, had carefully studied both films for evidence of tampering or trickery, but pronounced them both genuine.

Ball lightning, a rare atmospheric electrical phenomenon, was one suggested explanation. But the assembled scientists, all specialists in atmospheric plasma effects, rejected this.

Instead, they agreed with the opinion of Ron Strafford, Army munitions expert, that the objects filmed near Stonehenge were parachute-borne flares. Stonehenge, of course, is near the military ranges of Salisbury Plain.

The explanation for the Oxfordshire object turned out to be similarly prosaic. By reference to the size of trees on the horizon which it passed behind, the scientists estimated the UFO to be at least a mile from the camera and moving at several hundred miles an hour—too fast for ball lightning, but consistent with the speed of an aircraft, presumably one carrying a brilliant light which produced the luminous blob on the film.

When the aircraft light was switched off, the UFO vanished.

UFO: unidentified flying object

C HEART attacks tend to strike when the earth's magnetic activity is high, according to some remarkable results published last week.

The figures show a much closer correlation than would be expected by chance between variations in the magnetic field and the number of heart attack patients admitted to hospital in Hyderabad and Secunderabad, India.

On the face of it, the correlation is improbable. There seems no reason why small changes in the magnetic field, caused by variations in the number of charged particles emitted by the sun, could have anything to do with triggering heart attacks.

Nevertheless, the figures do show just such a correlation —'much to my astonishment,' admits Dr Stuart Malin of the Institute of Geological Sciences in Edinburgh, one of two authors of an article in last week's Nature.

Dr Malin assumes that the changes in magnetism are not the cause of heart attacks, though they could be the triggering factor which determines when a person predisposed to an attack actually has it.

He suggests, 'in a spirit of pure speculation,' that maybe the increase in magnetic field could induce electrical currents in a heart patient which were just sufficient to interfere with the natural 'pacemaker' signals which normally keep the heart going at the right speed.

D

PASADENA, Calif., March 7 (Reuters) — The Voyager-1 spacecraft has discovered a ring around the planet Jupiter, scientists reported today.

Dr. Bradford Smith, head of the Voyager-1 picture analysis team, said at the Jet Propulsion Laboratory here that the ring was made up of large particles which take about seven hours to circle Jupiter.

The ring, photographed by Voyager-1, was probably less than 30 kilometers thick and probably thousands of kilometers wide, he said.

E

A BREAKTHROUGH in the provision of energy from the sun for the countries of the European Community could be brought forward by up to two decades, given a modest increase in the Common Market's research effort in this field, according to the senior EEC scientists engaged in experiments in solar energy at EEC's scientific laboratories at Ispra, near Milan.

The senior West German scientist in charge of the Community's solar energy programme, Mr Joachim Gretz, told journalists that at present levels of research spending it was most unlikely that solar energy would provide even three per cent of the Community's energy requirements until after the year 2,000. But he said that with a five-fold increase in the present, modest sums, devoted by the Common Market to this work it was possible that the breakthrough could be achieved by the end of the next decade.

Mr Gretz calculates that if solar energy only provided three per cent of the EEC's needs, this could still produce a saving of about a billion pounds in the present bill for imported energy. And he believes that with new possibilities of converting solar energy into hydrogen thaat it might be possible to satisfy a much bigger share of the Community's future energy needs if seams were developed to exploit "sun spots" in southern Europe and the Alps as well as in African countries anxious for investment projects in energy with the Community.

At present the EEC spends about £2.6 millions a year on solar research at Ispra, one of the Common Market's official joint research centres, and another £3 millions a year in indirect research with universities and other independent bodies.

EEC: European Economic Community

39

F ASTRONOMERS believe that they have identified an enormous "black hole," five thousand million times the mass of the sun but invisible because its gravity is so powerful that no radiatiaon can escape from it, at the centre of our nearest active galaxy, M87.

The discovery, made by a team of scientists from University College, London, the University of Victoria, the Hale Observatory, and Kitt Peak National Observatory, could be crucial to progress in astronomy. It represents the first major observational evidence of the existence of massive "b l a c k h o l e" — objects which have been pos-tulated as a prime source of extremely high-energy processes in the universe.

In theory, "black holes" are the end product of burned out stars which undergo gravitational collapse and become super-dense. In that state they are invisible to normal observations because their enormously powerful gravitational field prevents the escape of detectable radiation. But their gravitational field attracts nearby matter and accelerates it so violently that enormously powerful secondary radiation is produced.

On existing theory, the enormous energy needed to drive the processes observed at the centres of distant galaxies could only be provided by "black holes" of gigantic mass. The new observation confirms the probable existence of these enormous concentrations of matter.

It was discovered that the light output of the centre of galaxy M87—which is about 65 million light years from Earth and about 100 times the size of our own galaxy—was far too high to be explained by normal theories of galactic structure.

This anomalous luminosity was studied by a highly sensitive spectroscopic device called an image photon counting system, which has been developed at University College,

4 Below are seven words and expressions taken from article B. In each case decide which of the four alternatives following the word or expression is most similar in meaning to it in the context of the article.   ⇒ page 100–D.

a) *back up*
   i)   destroy
   ii) improve
   iii) support
   iv) increase

b) *sceptics*
   i)   believers
   ii) scientists
   iii) experts
   iv) doubters

c) *countless*
   i)   very many
   ii) very few
   iii) ordinary
   iv) interesting

d) *luminous*
   i)   giving out light
   ii) strangely shaped
   iii) very large
   iv) moving

e) *hovering*
   i)   descending
   ii) flying
   iii) hanging
   iv) moving violently

f) *scrutiny*
   i)   discussion
   ii) disbelief
   iii) excitement
   iv) examination

g) *ranges*
   i)   buildings
   ii) shooting areas
   iii) camps
   iv) airfields

5 Decide which of the articles (excluding article B) on pages 38–40 most interests you. Read it very carefully, writing down any words or expressions which you do not know. Without looking at a dictionary try to work out the meaning of these words.   ⇒ page 100–D.

6 Divide into small groups. Each group is now the team of reporters responsible for producing a weekly radio science programme. This programme consists of headlines, followed by more detailed accounts of some of the week's science news. It also includes one or two interviews. You have already read the news content for this week (see preceding articles). Your job now is to convert it into a short lively radio programme.

6

COMMENT

1   On pages 42–4 you will find three editorials taken from the Comment section
    of three different newspapers.   ⇒ page 99–A.   Skim over the three editorials *as
    quickly as possible* in order to decide which editorial deals with the subject of
    a) the economic development of the poorest countries of the world;
    b) the place of women in the Church;
    c) the inadequacies of the British prison system.

2   On page 42 you will find the headlines which appeared with the editorials you have
    just looked at. Match the editorials and the headlines.

3   For each editorial write down
    a) the news event which gave rise to the editorial;
    b) the opinion or main conclusion of the editorial.

4   Your aim in this exercise is to scan the editorials quickly in order to find the answers
    to the questions below. Do not worry about detail that is not directly related to the
    information you are looking for. Before beginning to read Editorial A, read the first
    question for that editorial. Quickly scan the editorial and underline the word, phrase,
    or sentence which answers the question. Repeat for all the questions.   ⇒ page 99–B.

EDITORIAL A
According to the editorial
a) Who will be disappointed by the recent decision of the Anglican clergy?
b) What should the first aim of Christians be?
c) What has contributed to the demand for women priests?

EDITORIAL B
According to the editorial
a) What is the first duty of government?
b) What is the ratio of prisoners to guards in British prisons?
c) What will happen on 5 November?
d) What is the writer referring to when he mentions 'Gartree' and 'Nottingham'?
e) Which European country has the biggest prison population?
f) How long ago were most of the prisons built?
g) What is the effect of imprisonment on most inmates?
h) What kind of punishments should be given to
      – rapists?
        habitual drunkards?
      – young violent offenders?
      – con-men?

According to the editorial

a) What is the purpose of economic development in the poorest parts of the world?
b) When was the World Bank's annual meeting held?
c) How many people in the poor countries are living in absolute poverty?
d) Who is Robert McNamara?
e) What is the total population of the poor countries?
f) What was life expectancy in a country like Indonesia in 1960?
g) In which ways has the quality of life improved in the poorest countries of the world over the last 15 to 20 years?
h) What do the poorest countries of the world most need from the industrial world?

¹ Punishment without degradation in our prisons

² A victory for tradition

³ World Bank and World's Poor

EDITORIAL A

BY REJECTING women priests the Anglican clergy have stood up for the traditional way in which the Church of England is run.

All conservatives, be they Christian or not, can take some comfort from this fact. The decision will come as a great disappointment to those women who have felt the call to serve God in the priesthood.

But we are entitled to ask : Would they have felt such a call but for the emergence of "women's liberation"? We doubt it. The Church, which stands at the intersection of time and eternity, never should be a slave to fashion.

Moreover, all Christians must agree that Christian re-unification ought to be a primary aim. The fact is that the ordination of women would, because of the strongly held view of Rome, put off this great prospect in aid of a minor concession to contemporary fashion. It is not worth it. The Anglican clergy were right.

from *Daily Express*

WHATEVER else a government may seek to undertake, its duty to keep order in civil society, uphold the law and punish wrongdoers is paramount.

It is a grave indictment of the present Government, which has assumed more responsibilities than any other in our country's peacetime history, that it should have let the prison service drift into neglect bordering on chaos. Both prisoners and their custodians are in a mutinous fury.

Prisoners outnumber guards by three to one, and it is surprising there have not been more riots. Allegations of beatings and heavy sedation by drugs point to a breakdown of conventional authority.

On November 5 prison officers at 30 or 40 places are to begin disruptive tactics in pursuit of an overtime claim which could require governors to bring in armed troops in their place. The rebellions of inmates at Gartree, earlier this month, and at Nottingham — both maximum-security establishments — raise the spectre of overt hostilities, even killings, when the Army arrives.

The blame should not be laid solely on Labour's head. It is axiomatic among politicians that there are no votes to be gained by spending money on prisons. The seeds of today's imminent breakdown in penal discipline were sown long ago; and they were allowed to flourish both by permissive social reformers and by law-and-order exponents.

Our prison population, Europe's largest, is housed, for the most part appallingly, in antiquated fortress-slums, overcrowded in a way their Victorian architects, stern though they were, never foresaw. Locked for long hours in cells with nothing to do but compare notes and mimic their extra-mural hierarchies and rivalries, it is no wonder that criminals are only hardened and confirmed in villainy by imprisonment.

Congestion breeds tension: not till prisons are emptied of many classes of convict can they be pacified constructively. The rule should be that only criminals who pose a constant danger to others—robbers-with-violence, rapists, terrorists, gang leaders—should be incarcerated.

For recidivists such as habitual drunkards, who are more pathetic than menacing, a form of halfway house between freedom and imprisonment must be devised with a firm but supportive regimen. For young thugs and vandals, a glasshouse régime must be tried which prevents their corruption by confirmed criminals. And for non-violent offenders such as fraudulent converters and con-men, a punishment which involves restitution to society but not isolation from it is best.

Britain should adopt a penal policy which acknowledges that different law - breakers are driven by different motives. Most cannot be rehabilitated by banishment to a university of crime. Nor can the prison officer's status be raised while he is forced to rely on the cosh, the chamber pot and the syringe. They dignify their user no more than their victim. All this will cost us money; but it will be an investment in peace and security for us all.

from *Evening Standard*

glasshouse: a military detention centre
con-men: men who trick, cheat and defraud others
cosh: heavy stick

The purpose of economic development in the poorest regions of the world is not to be found in the rows of statistics on production and trade. It lies in the opportunity to improve the chances that new-born infants will survive, that they will go to school and learn to read, that they will live longer than their parents, that they will spend those years in communities more hopeful than the slums now growing uncontrollably around the tropical cities. The World Bank's annual meeting, held here last week, is an occasion for taking stock of conditions among the rich and the poor. The bank itself, as the major conduit of development capital from north to south, has also become the leading source of reliable comparative information on subjects reaching far beyond finance.

By the end of this century, if things continue on their present course, there will be 600 million people around the world living in absolute poverty, at the edge of survival. That forecast was offered by the president of the bank, Robert McNamara, as an indicator of need. Taken by itself, the number raises a certain danger that Americans will respond by merely throwing up their hands at the impossibility of doing anything at all about need on such a scale. But Mr. McNamara was making the opposite point: Things are demonstrably changing and improving in most of the poor countries. By the bank's count, about 800 million people — just under two-fifths of the total populations — are now living in absolute poverty in those countries. If the number drops to 600 million over the next generation, it will mean that the proportion has fallen to less than one-fifth. If so much can be accomplished with the present rather modest amounts of aid and government-backed lending, does that not become an urgent argument for doing more?

There are some three dozen countries — India and Indonesia are the largest among them — in which economic output per capita is less than $250 a year. Out of every 1,000 babies born there, 122 die before their first birthday. That's eight times the rate in the United States. But it's down from the 1960 rate of 144. Life expectancy there is about 44 years (compared with 73 currently in the United States), but that's up from 36 years in 1960. Also since 1960, literacy in this those countries has almost doubled; one out of every four persons now can read, and among young children half are going to school. Only one out of 12 goes on to high school, but 15 years ago it was one out of 50. One family out of every four now has access to a safe water supply.

But the savage arithmetic of population growth continues as usual. Although death rates are down significantly in those parts of the world, birth rates are not. There has been substantial improvement in several big countries, but there's no general pattern. Nearly half of this population is under the age of 15. The proportion living in the cities is still low — about one out of every eight people — but it's rising fast. Food production per capita in those poorest countries is a little lower now than it was a decade ago.

Over the turbulent years from 1970 to 1975 — the years of oil crisis and crop failure — it was generally the middle range of developing countries whose economies expanded most rapidly. The rich industrial economies proved more vulnerable and did less well. But it was the poorest countries whose economic growth rates were lowest of all in those years.

Those countries need two things, above all else, from the industrial world. They need access to markets, and that access is reduced every time a country like the United States puts quotas and restrictions on its imports of their products. They also need capital. That is why the World Bank is now asking its sponsors and donors, the governments of the rich countries, to increase its lending capacity. In relation to the size of its own growing economy, the United States is now contributing just half as much as it did in 1960.

from *The Washington Post*

5   Divide into groups with three or four people in each. Choose the editorial which most interests you and discuss it. At the end of your discussion, report back to the whole class, outlining the different points of view expressed, and any conclusions reached by the group.

6   Choose one of the editorials and write a letter to the Editor of the newspaper, stating your own views.

7

LETTERS TO THE EDITOR

Section A

1   Decide whether or not you agree with the following statements.
    a) There is nothing to be said in defence of smoking. It is unpleasant, unnecessary and dangerous.
    b) Today's society does not provide enouth facilities (e.g. cinema, youth clubs, sport etc.) for teenagers.
    c) Women should not go out to work if they have children.
    d) Prisoners should be made to work in a prison factory and earn money.
    e) Capital punishment reduces crime.
    f) It is sometimes appropriate and not necessarily harmful for parents to hit or smack their children.

2   Read the letters on pages 45–7. The letters discuss the same topics as the statements in exercise 1. Beside each letter, write the number of the statement which corresponds to it.   ⇒ page 99–A.

3   Decide whether the writer of each letter agrees with your own point of view.

4   Divide into groups and discuss the topic(s) which most interests you. Make a list of points for and against each question. Report back to the class.

5   Choose the letter which most interests you and write a letter of reply.

UNDER 18 PLATFORM

Where can we teenagers go?

I AM writing to complain about the lack of facilities for teenagers in my town. The cinema has just closed and I have to go 10 miles to the nearest one.

There are no youth clubs near me and I have to stay in at night and get bored. Mum moans at me for getting under her feet. I am sure other teenagers share my complaint.

All teenagers are labelled hooligans but only a few are vandals. Teenagers only become vandals because of the lack of things to do.

A lot more youth clubs, a disco every Saturday night, and football and cricket teams should be organised. Vandals, as well as being fined, should be banned from these activities for six months.
                    CHRIS BEAL (15),
                    Hitchin, Herts.

Good sense from a Russian prison

From the Earl of HUNTINGDON

SIR—During the 1930s I was fortunate in being shown round a Russian prison — not political, but for ordinary criminals.

The whole concept seemed to be much better than that of the prisons in this country. After a spell with good behaviour in a Moscow prison, a prisoner could be transferred to a commune which was run as a factory.

The prisoner worked daily, earning a wage, part of which he could save for when his term was over or send back to his family. The prisoners, as far as one could judge, seemed to be reasonably contented; the prison staff were fully occupied in looking after the prison, the prisoners, and running the factory.

For bad behaviour a prisoner could be put in solitary confinement, which meant that he was not allowed to leave his hut for a period. In cases of seriously disruptive behaviour the prisoner was called before a monthly prison meeting, and publicly berated. I was told that this rarely happened to a prisoner twice.

The advantages of the system seemed to be that the prisoners were kept fully occupied, were trained in jobs which could be useful to them after they were released, and that the prison officers seemed to be busy and contented. Above, all, the goods from the factory paid all and sometimes more than the expenses of the prison.

I know that the trade unions in Britain are against such a scheme since they fear that, beneficial as it might be for prisoners and for reducing crime, it would take away jobs from other workers at a time when unemployment is drastically high.

I believe that this view is based on a fallacy which is that this country with its population and resources can produce only a certain amount of goods. Actually, with proper encouragement, better co-operation and more skilful management I feel sure we could produce far more and of a quality that would sell even in times of depression. Also the money saved in running our prisons could be very profitably used.

Crime and prisons are a serious problem. Could we not try an experiment on Russian lines?

HUNTINGDON
Beaulieu, Hants.

The shame of hanging

THERE seems to have been a good deal of baying from some sections of society for the return of hanging.

I was a Federal hangman in Malaya from 1946-48. It was a time of military executions for war and terrorist crimes and I was involved in 143 executions.

Capital punishment is nothing short of legalised murder. It is not an answer to crimes of violence.

I wonder how many of those who advocate the return of capital punishment would be prepared to carry it out? The preparation and aftermath of this act of shame is horrific. I speak from experience.—W. P. Hayes, Middx.

What a carry on for working mums

I DO not agree with Mrs Bonnick of Kent, who says mothers of young children should not go out to work.

Does she not realise that many young couples could not otherwise afford to have children?

Surely she cannot expect such couples to remain childless victims of the present economic climate.

Mothers should ignore non-constructive criticism and carry on doing what they personally think is best for the family.

(Mrs) DIANA L. DYSON,
Ossett, West Yorkshire.

a carry on: a fuss, commotion

YEAR OF THE CHILD

Sir, — Children constitute the largest oppressed minority on the planet. Even in the event of the liberation of all other minorities (economic, national, sexual, racial) there will still remain the difficult and subtle task of the emancipation of children. But not until then will h'mankind have established the only possible basis for freedom and happiness for all.

Corporal punishment in schools and in the family is one of the means by which a society, through certain significant adult figures, moulds, frightens and controls the young life that it needs to reproduce its structures. Perhaps it is not any more the more widely used one; and certainly it's not the more sophisticated. Psychological manipulation is less obviously repugnant and probably deeper in its effects. Yet, to beat a child *is* an insulting, cruel, humiliating and destructive thing to do and this, irrespective of its 'good' or 'bad' long-term consequences, should be enough to condemn it. It also expresses the unconscious hatred of the body that still pervades countries with a strong Christian tradition. Children in holy Ireland are still split from their primary objects of interest and pleasure, their bodies. The sexes are educated apart, in ignorance and fear of each other, interest in masturbation is fiercely condemned or diverted away through some psychological trick. Instead of a sexual life the children are offered, if they are very lucky, a sexual "education" given by some probable virgin in a boring, fleshless, pseudo-scientific style.

Not corporal punishment but corporal love should be the guiding force in education. Only when a child is allowed to love and accept his total being can he grow into a sane and free individual. Otherwise his emotions *and* his intellect will be damaged.

I would like to see more individuals, organisations and, best of all, the children themselves coming together to put an end to this shame once and for all, not because 1979 will be the so-called Year of the Child but because it's a good and urgent change to bring about.— Yours, etc.,

JUAN CAMPOS
14 Eugene Street,
Dublin 8.

Benefits of smoking

From Mr Winston Fletcher

Sir, The essential fact about smoking, which your correspondents and most other commentators of recent years seem to have ignored, is that cigarettes give a vast number of people a good deal of pleasure a lot of the time. That is why the world smoked almost 5,000,000,000,000 of them last year; approximately 1,200 for every man, woman and child on earth.

It is not high pressure advertising that makes the Chinese smoke heavily —any more than it was wicked merchants who persuaded the seventeenth century Persians to smoke, despite the Shah's ingenious punishment of pouring molten lead down their throats when they were caught.

There is considerable evidence, surprisingly little publicized by the cigarette manufacturers, that smoking produces certain beneficial effects in human beings. Frankenhaeuser, et al (Stockholm, 1971) showed that smoking counteracts the decrease in efficiency that typically occurs in boring, monotonous situations. The same team (1972) showed that smokers improved their performance in complex choice situations, while smoking. There is a growing body of evidence that nicotine can produce a tranquilizing effect during high emotional and shock situations, while on the other hand stimulating concentration and mental effort in tedious, somnific situations.

None of which proves that smoking may cause cancer or other illnesses. But the evidence clearly establishes that smoking is by no means an unmitigated evil, against which no benefits can be set. On the contrary, the benefits of smoking may be considerable: in 1957 the late Sir Compton Mackenzie wrote: "If cigarettes vanished from the earth today, I believe the world would go to war again within a comparatively short lapse of time."

An extravagant exaggeration, perhaps. But certainly tempers would be shorter, nastier, and more brutish.

Yours faithfully,
WINSTON FLETCHER,
Souldern Mill,
Bicester.
Oxfordshire.

Section B

I Below you will find six letters which were written to a newspaper in response to a letter or article which had previously appeared in the newspaper. ⇒ page 99–B. Fill in the frame below, showing where possible
a) whether the letter is in response to a letter or an article;
b) the name of the person who wrote the original letter or article;
c) the subject matter;
d) whether the writer of the letter you are reading agrees with the previous writer.

Letter	In answer to letter or article	Name of previous writer	Subject matter	Agree/Disagree
A				
B				
C				
D				
E				
F				

A I WAS interested to read in the "Under 18" column a letter from a young man saying that if school leavers had not found a job within 18 months they should be drafted into the Services.

From my son's experience I can recommend Service life.

He was a typical 17-year-old when he joined the RAF with long hair and scruffy jeans and I felt sure the first time a sergeant shouted at him he would shout back. Not a bit of it. A few weeks ago, I stood in a freezing aircraft hangar proudly watching his passing-out parade.

The transformation in just six weeks was unbelievable. His entire manner and bearing have changed. He loves the life and is on the threshold of a sound and interesting career.

(Mrs) JANETTE
HARDY-CARR,
Brighton, East Sussex.

the Services: army, navy and air force
RAF: Royal Air Force

B IN AN article on pop stars who die young, Judith Simons re-states the view of drummer Ginger Baker that "most musicians are ravers —people who like to live it up—with a strong self-destructive streak."

Most pop performers are not musicians but hysterics, out to engender a similar hysteria in their audiences.

They have no voices and little knowledge of the possibilities of the instruments they play, the guitarists able and content to do barely more than slap out a few basic cords.

The dedication which music demands in technique, application and memory is something very different. Pianists, composers, singers and violinists pursuing this course mostly live long.

You don't become a Rubinstein or a Heifetz by being a raver.

DAVID BRANSON,
Hastings, East Sussex.

C

It is ironic yet illuminating that David Haworth's article (IHT, Feb. 27) about dissension in the Netherlands over abortion should only have quoted the male premier, the male finance minister, one male bishop, the male pope, one male cardinal, one male adviser and one male poet.

The unstated assumption here is that it is only natural such an issue should be decided by *men*. Wrong: Women alone should have the right to decide what is done with their own bodies.

A (male) journalist's treatment of abortion as a struggle between church and state distorts the real issue: enforced motherhood. Whether determined by church *or* state, this is a crime against women. Disagreement between groups of men as to which one should control women's bodies simply compounds this crime.

LYDIA W. HORTON.

E

HAVING read Clare Dover's report on the pointlessly cruel experiments carried out on animals by psychologists, of all people, I must write and say how much I agree with the views of Dr Alice Heim.

As anyone who has ever had a pet cat or dog will know, many animals are capable of feeling both emotion and pain.

Use of mammals for medical purposes can probably be justified. But can we as a society, which prides itself on its intelligence and compassion, continue to allow the use of animals for cosmetic research, or for the mere pursuit of abstract knowledge, when that knowledge can have no foreseeable advantage for mankind ?

CAROL ATKINSON.
Meopham, Kent.

F

REFERRING to a recently published letter about the violent attack on Constable Merry, I feel I must write to you. As a policeman's wife I would hate to think of my husband going to work wearing a gun, as your correspondent suggested.

Violence is very bad now. But can you imagine the sort of violence there would be if policemen were made to wear guns ? Villains would always feel they would have to go one better with weapons in order to come out on top.

I would not like to see this country become like America. People from all over the world say : " British police are wonderful." That's how we want it to stay.

I know, my husband would leave the police force rather than carry firearms.

(Mrs) I. GURNEY,
Chessington, Surrey.

D

ALCOHOLISM comes in people, not in bottles. Jill Tweedie is mistaken, I think, if she expects laws and prices to be effective against a compulsive illness, Prohibition vastly increased the .social costs of drinking in America. Only a very small percentage of the population are alcoholics, and what is effective is Alcoholics Anonymous.

That was how I managed to stop drinking and to stay stopped, happily, for the past 16 years. One of the delusions I got rid of, which had hindered me from admitting my problem, was that my capacity for drink was a measure of my manhood.

Sober, I have found it both unworkable and unnecessary to make up stories about why I am not drinking alcohol. Most people are almost exclusively interested in what is in their own glass, not mine.
— Yours faithfully,

J.C.

London.

Alcoholics Anonymous: organisation which helps alcoholics

2 Divide into small groups. Choose the letter which most interests you. Make sure you have looked at it in detail and understand it.

3 In your groups discuss the subject matter of the letter you have chosen. Prepare an oral report of your discussion for the rest of the class. Your report should include
   – the point of view expressed in the letter;
   – the different points of view expressed by the members of the group;
   the general conclusions you reached.

4 Write a letter of reply to the Editor of the newspaper.

8

MOTORING NEWS ▌

Section A

1 Below and on page 51 you will find six articles and the headlines which appeared with them. Match the articles and the headlines.   ⇒ page 99–A.

2 Scan the same articles in order to answer the following questions. Do not worry about detail that is not directly related to the information you are looking for. Before reading each article read the first question for that article carefully. Quickly scan the article for the answer. Underline the word, phrase or sentence which answers the question. Repeat for all the questions.   ⇒ page 99–B.

ARTICLE A
a) What percentage of deaths on French roads were caused by drunken driving?
b) Where were 506 motorists given the breath test last week?
c) How many of the 506 motorists failed the breath test?
d) Who is suffering as a result of the new law?

ARTICLE B
a) When did US policemen first begin to use radar to catch speeding drivers?
b) Who was pleased by Judge Nesbitt's decision?

ARTICLE C
a) Which car firm is introducing the buzzer?
b) How many engineering improvements is the firm introducing on its 1979 models?
c) When will the buzzer go off?

ARTICLE D
a) How many traffic wardens were injured last year?
b) What are the wardens usually doing when they are injured?

1 *U.S. Car-Repair Report Indicates Rampant Incompetence, Gouging*

2 **Buzzer you can't forget**

3 **Traffic meters spring a trap**

4 **Swiss Voters Turn Down Ban on Sunday Traffic**

5 *Radar No Proof Of Car's Speed, U.S. Judge Says*

6 **MON DIEU!**

A

In the 1950s, French Prime Minister Pierre Mendès-France tried to persuade his countrymen to switch from wine to milk. Now, with somewhat more success, French authorities are trying to turn motorists into teetotalers. Armed with a tough new law against drunken driving—the cause of 40 per cent of the fatalities on French highways in 1977—police may stop a motorist at any time for a breath test. Serious infractions of the law may cost a driver his license for as long as six years.

Last week, police zeroed in on Paris's busy Place de la Concorde and in one afternoon administered breath tests to 506 motorists (all of whom passed). The new law may reduce the mayhem on France's highways, but many restaurant proprietors bemoan its effects on their business—and on gourmet traditions. One Paris restaurateur fumed: "Today, I had to serve mineral water with my pâté de foie gras. Sacrilege!"

zero in on: to focus attention on, attack

B

MIAMI, May 8 (NYT) — A Miami judge ruled yesterday that radar is an inexact and often unreliable instrument of law enforcement.

Judge Alfred Nesbitt of Metropolitan Dade County Court, after two weeks of challenges to police radar procedures to catch speeding motorists, said that he no longer would convict accused traffic violators on the basis of radar evidence alone.

While the ruling had no immediate legal effect outside his own courtroom, Judge Nesbitt said that he felt other judges might be influenced by it.

Those critics who have waged an attack on radar as a "capricious and arbitrary" tool of law enforcement hailed the ruling as the first victory against radar technology since it was placed in the hands of the nation's traffic policemen a generation ago.

C

A CAR firm has come to the rescue of absent-minded motorists with a buzzer that sounds if they leave their lights on after parking.

It will also save them from locking their keys in the car, by sounding before the door can be shut if the ignition key is left in.

Volvo are fitting the buzzer on the new 2·7, 2·1, and 2-litre series. It is among more than 800 engineering improvements to the Swedish firm's 1979 models which will cost between 5 and 6 per cent. more than last year.

They include, on 2·1s, a restyled front grille ; headlights with wash-wipe units and polished cast aluminium bumpers.

The V-six models get improved suspension systems for better road holding and the 2·7 litre engine has a redesigned induction system,

D

TRAFFIC wardens in London are threatening industrial action because they are facing a growing number of physical assaults — from parking meters.

At least 84 wardens were injured by the meters last year and many have had to receive hospital treatment for broken fingers and thumbs. Others have come away with only scratched hands and faces.

.The cause appears to be a spring in the winding mechanism of the meters which has a nasty habit of snapping in the fingers or face of the unfortunate warden when he is rewinding them.

E

WASHINGTON, May 8 (UPI) — An undercover survey of auto-repair shops shows that the U.S. consumer has "only about a 50-50 chance of getting a car fixed right and for the right price," Transportation Secretary Brock Adams said yesterday.

The survey showed that more than half of the $50 billion U.S. customers spend every year on car repairs — 53 cents of each dollar — goes for needless work.

The biggest problem, he said, is engine repair, where it is "almost a sure thing" that the work will not be done properly.

"When we took test cars into repair shops at random," Mr. Adams said, "we found that what we have . . . is a variety of wasteful practices, including habitual overrepair or package deals — and just plain old lack of competence to do the job right."

The survey found that the chances the shops would fix something that did not need fixing were 25 percent in the case of brakes, 19 percent for suspensions, 78 percent for engines and 39 percent overall, Mr. Adams said. He added that the chances of the shops' failing to correct real problems were 11 percent for brakes, 31 percent for suspensions, 28 percent for engines and 21 percent overall.

The survey was conducted at 62 dealerships, service stations and independent repair shops in Atlanta, Philadelphia, Miami, Nashville, Houston, New York and White Plains, N.Y. The shops were not identified, but Mr. Adams said that the information is being turned over to local law enforcement officials. He noted that survey agents of both sexes had been gouged about equally.

F

Swiss voters today overwhelmingly rejected a student-initiated proposal to ban all motorized traffic, including cars driven by foreign tourists, on the second Sunday of every month.

The motion was defeated by a 2-to-1 margin. In some areas dependent on tourist income it was three-to-one against.

The government had warned, before the national referendum, that approval of the motion would represent a violation of individual liberty and would be economically and politically disastrous.

Hotels, restaurants, summer and winter resorts would all suffer, the government said, and Switzerland's neighbors would hardly be happy if hundreds of thousands of their nationals found Swiss border crossings closed down on 12 Sundays a year.

a) Who is Brock Adams?
b) How much do US customers spend every year on car repairs?
c) What kind of repair is most frequently not done properly?

ARTICLE F
a) Who originally proposed that motoring should be banned on certain Sundays in Switzerland?
b) What was the Swiss government's attitude towards the proposition?
c) What was the reasoning behind the government's attitude?

3 Divide into small groups and discuss the following questions. Be prepared to report back to the whole class giving reasons for your opinions and conclusions.
a) Do you think that drunken driving is a serious offence? How is it punished in your country? How do you think it should be punished?
b) Is radar used by traffic police in your country? How far do you agree with Judge Nesbitt that 'radar is an inexact and often unreliable instrument of law enforcement'? How else might speeding drivers be detected? How is speeding punished in your country?
c) Is traffic a serious problem in your country? How difficult is it to find a place to park your car? Are parking meters used in your country? If so, how does the system work? If not, what methods are used to control congestion in cities?
d) Have you ever had the experience of taking your car to be repaired and the job not being done properly? Do you think it happens often? Repairs constitute only one of the expenses car owners have. What are the others?

4 Read the article 'Safety meeting backs seat belt campaign'. Decide whether the following statements are true or false according to the information contained in the article.

Safety meeting backs seat belt campaign

Government plans to make the wearing of vehicle seat belts compulsory won support yesterday at a safety conference, but only after disagreements.

The arguments for and against a strict seat-belt law were heard at the Royal Society for the Prevention of Accidents' annual conference at Bournemouth.

Delegates refused to vote on the direct issue, but backed by a majority of two to one a motion calling for legislation to ensure road users comply with measures "for their own safety".

Lord Nugent of Guildford, a former Minister for Transport and the society's deputy president, said: "The wearing of seat belts for the driver and front passenger is a safety measure of such fundamental value for saving life and limb that it should be backed by the law".

But Lord Lucas of Chilworth said: "Compulsion hits at the very fundamentals of democracy".

from *The Times*

a) The government has passed a law making the wearing of seat belts compulsory.
b) Delegates at the Royal Society for the Prevention of Accidents' conference voted against the use of seat belts.
c) Lord Nugent used to be Minister for Transport.
d) Lord Nugent is in favour of making seat belts compulsory.
e) Lord Lucas is in favour of making seat belts compulsory.

5 Imagine you have read the article about seat belts in your newspaper, and as you feel very strongly on this subject you write a letter to the newspaper. In the letter refer to the article and state your own views on the subject.

Section B

1 Read the article 'Hazard food ahead' on page 54. Below are ten words and expressions taken from the article. In each case decide which of the four alternatives following the word or expression is most similar in meaning to it in the context of the article.
⇒ page 100–D.

a) *hazards*
   i) service areas
   ii) advantages
   iii) dangers
   iv) expenses

b) *pull off*
   i) enter
   ii) leave
   iii) lift
   iv) take away

c) *liable to*
   i) will probably
   ii) will never
   iii) would like to
   iv) will certainly

d) *soggy*
   i) soft
   ii) frozen
   iii) hard
   iv) cold

e) *stewed*
   i) fresh
   ii) cold
   iii) tasteless
   iv) not freshly made

f) *overpriced*
   i) of bad quality
   ii) smelling bad
   iii) too expensive
   iv) too cheap

g) *scourge*
   i) admirer
   ii) friend
   iii) eater
   iv) critic

h) *pull our socks up*
   i) behave politely
   ii) dress well
   iii) improve
   iv) stop eating

i) *hard-up*
   i) angry
   ii) poor
   iii) drunk
   iv) cruel

j) *overshot*
   i) drove into
   ii) drove away from
   iii) drove through
   iv) drove past

Hazard food ahead

AMONG the hazards facing motorway travellers is FOOD. And that's official.

When a driver pulls off the road into a service area, he is liable to run into soggy chips, overcooked peas, stewed tea, and tasteless ham in damp bread.

According to a committee appointed by the Government to investigate motorway services, up to 60 per cent. of meals are sub-standard and overpriced.

In some cases, it seems, staff can't tell the difference between good and bad food.

In their report yesterday, the "watchdogs" revealed that the worst dish they tasted was steak and kidney pie.

By MARK DOWDNEY

Failed

Later, when they introduced themselves to the catering manager involved, he pointed to the pie with genuine pride.

"Look at that," he said. "That is what Egon Ronay [food writer and scourge of motorway cooking] thought was dreadful."

More than half the cafeterias, transport cafes and restaurants in service areas failed to meet quality standards set by consultants employed by the committee.

The members of the committee, headed by Bulmer's Cider chairman Peter Prior, included the Daily Mirror consumer affairs writer Margaret Jones.

Already the Government has accepted their main recommendation—that Whitehall should take a smaller cut of motorway service area profits in an attempt to help raise standards.

Transport Minister William Rodgers said yesterday: "The message of this report is that we must all pull our socks up."

The inquiry team found that most of the thirty-nine service areas didn't make excessive profits. Twelve lost money last year.

Deal

One of the public's biggest complaints is about the cost of petrol. The committee recommended a new deal to cut the price by up to 8p a gallon.

Other improvements urged by the committee are banks in service areas and picnic spots where travellers can eat their own food. Motorway workers singled out for praise by the report include petrol attendant Joe Cookson, who has lent cash to many hard-up motorists.

Samaritan Joe, 64, works at the Forton service station near Lancaster.

He said last night: "It began with a doctor in a Jaguar who overshot Manchester and didn't have enough petrol to get back. I lent him £2·50 and he sent me back £3 and a lovely letter.

"Since then I have helped out well over fifty people."

from *Daily Mirror*

watchdog: inspector, guardian against illegal practices
Whitehall: the administrative centre of government in Britain
cut: percentage, part
Samaritan: somebody who helps people in trouble

2   Decide whether the following statements are true or false according to the article 'Hazard food ahead'.
  a) More than half of motorway service meals are unsatisfactory according to a recent Government report.
  b) Motorway staff agree that meals on motorways could be better.
  c) Peter Prior works for the *Daily Mirror*.
  d) The Government has rejected the report.

e) Some motorway service areas lose money.

f) The committee praised all services, other than food, provided by motorway service areas.

g) The Forton service station is not far from Manchester.

3 Divide into small groups and discuss the following questions. Be prepared to report back to the whole class giving reasons for your opinions and conclusions.

a) The motorway service areas described in the article are English. What do you think of the motorway service areas in your own country and other countries you have visited?

b) What are the advantages and disadvantages of motorway travelling? Which way do you prefer to travel?

"Thank heaven for that."

from *Punch*

Section C

Look at the article 'Boys' invalid car catches EEC eye' in order to answer the following questions. Work as quickly as possible. Do not worry about detail that is not directly related to the information you are looking for.   ⇒ page 99–B.

a) Who designed the car?
b) Where might the car become the standard car for the disabled?
c) Who is Mr Alf Morris?
d) What is the name of the car?
e) Who is Mr Barber?
f) Which three major groups are showing interest in the car?

Boys' invalid car catches EEC eye

A CAR for disabled people, designed by boys at Shrewsbury School, is being considered as a standard vehicle for use throughout the Common Market. Its main feature is that the disabled driver can enter the car and drive it away without getting out of a wheelchair.

Consultants engaged by the British Steel Corporation are conducting a study of the possibility of redundant steel workers and plant being switched to production of the vehicle. The design has been considered by officials of Mr Alf Morris, Minister for the disabled, and in Brussels it has been suggested that the basic body concept could be regarded as standard throughout the EEC, with locally marketed engines used to power it.

The idea developed when a group of six boys aged 14 to 17 and their head of craft and design, Mr E. T. Barber, decided to enter the BP Buildacar competition for schools.

Mr Barber said : " The BP competition is basically for a car suitable for town use, but the boys decided to extend this and create a specialist car for disabled people. We discussed the problems with the local disabled drivers' association and decided that the most difficult situation for those who are severely disabled is transferring from the wheelchair to the car, then dragging the chair in after them."

The team overcame this by building a car with a nearside entrance incorporating a ramp which folds down to the pavement. The driver moves the wheelchair into the car, and behind the steering wheel.

Mr Barber said that the boys, who have called the car the Invashrew, were aware that a major disdvantage of the standard Ministry car still in use was that it could not carry passengers. They wanted to design a family car

Foot and hand controls have been incorporated in the prototype, although one or the other would be installed to suit the particular driver.

Mr Barber said : " The interest which is being shown by the British Steel group, the Ministry and the EEC is very exciting for the boys. All the work has been done in their own time."

from *The Guardian*

BP: British Petroleum (oil company)

Section D

1   Read the instructions for the safety contest 'Keep those kids happy and safe' and then fill in the form.

2   Divide into small groups and compare your answers. Discuss the reasons for your choices.

Keep those kids happy —and safe

ON every car journey you want your child to be safe. At the same time, as every parent knows, youngsters get bored and restless in the car, especially on long journeys.

Now there is a new answer to both of these problems.

It is a brand new concept in child safety, acting in the same way as a seat belt protecting your child in the event of an accident, and providing a play surface for a whole range of activities that will keep the youngster happy and occupied.

It has been designed for children aged between four and 10, and consists of a rear lap belt which straps around a moulded body restraint, and keeps the child securely and comfortably in the seat.

It stops the child from being thrown forward and sideways, and in the event of severe impact, the table compresses to absorb the shock and minimise injury.

When you haven't got children in the car, you simply lift the table out and the belt can be used on its own as a safety belt for adults.

JOURNEY

The Daily Express got together with Britax who designed the new Play Safe belt and came up with this contest on the theme of keeping children happy and contented on a car journey.

And there's a major prize of a Fiat Mirafiori 4-door saloon. Painted yellow with a black side stripe (the house colours of Britax) this car is fitted with the Weathershields Sunliner all-steel sliding roof.

There will be three Play Safes each day for the duration of the contest as consolation prizes.

ALL YOU HAVE TO DO :—

Suppose you are taking two children on a holiday which involves a long car journey. Listed below are eight other things you might do to keep them happy and contented while fitted in their Play Safes. Study them carefully, use your skill and judgment to place them in the order to ensure this.

For example, if you consider: "Ensure car is well ventilated" to be most important, place the letter "C" against "1st" on the entry form and so on for the eight features. Now add an extra idea of your own which we have not included. This will only be considered in the event of a tie for any of the prizes.

Judges will award the Mirafiori to the sender of the best overall entry. The three daily prizes will be awarded to the three best entries on each numbered coupon. In the event of a tie for any of the prizes, the extra "idea" will be considered to determine the outright winner.

You pay for one entry only —the rest are free. The total entry fee for this contest is 20p. For this you may send in as many entries as you wish providing they are on entry forms cut from the Daily Express and are all contained in one envelope. Plain paper entries and permutations will not be considered. Send your entries with a 20p postal order or cheque, to :

Daily Express "Play Safe" Contest, 4 Racquet Court, London, EC4X 1BB (Comp.).

to reach us not later than Wednesday, September 27.

Competitors, who must not be under 18 years of age, will be bound by the conditions of entry. Employees, and their relatives, of Express Newspapers may not take part in this contest, and no correspondence can be entered into.

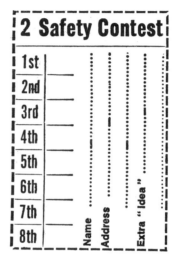

2 Safety Contest	Name	Address	Extra "idea"
1st			
2nd			
3rd			
4th			
5th			
6th			
7th			
8th			

HERE'S WHERE YOU CHOOSE

A Drive at leisure and allow ample time to reach your destination.

B Adult passenger to point out and discuss places of interest.

C Ensure car is well ventilated.

D Encourage children to play

spotting or "Spy" type of games.

E Plan a picnic on route.

H Ensure children are suitably clothed for journey.

J Allow sufficient stops for comfort.

K Choose interesting route.

---

from *Daily Express*

brand new : completely new

9

TRAVEL NEWS ▆▆▆▆▆▆▆▆▆▆

Section A

1 Look at the articles on page 59. ⇒ page 99–A. In one minute decide which article describes
   a) the complaints of air hostesses;
   b) a plane journey around the world;
   c) a failed hijack;
   d) the danger of malaria to travellers;
   e) a journey through the snow.

2 By scanning the articles, find the answers to the following questions as quickly as possible. Do not worry about detail that is not directly related to the information you are looking for. ⇒ page 99–B.

ARTICLE A
a) Who took 12 days $3\frac{1}{2}$ hours to fly round the world?
b) In which month did Jack Rodd break the record for flying round the world in a single-engine aircraft?

ARTICLE B
a) Where was the KLM jet going?
b) Why did Paul Gooker try to hijack the jet?

ARTICLE C
a) What nationality is Naomi Uemura?
b) How long is Greenland?
c) How often does the Nimbus-6 satellite fly over the pole during the expedition?
d) When did Mr Uemura begin his trip?

ARTICLE D
a) How old is Miss Benedikte Kaalund?
b) Who is Miss Katy Morgan?
c) When do the majority of aircraft accidents occur?

ARTICLE E
a) What is the worst kind of malaria?
b) Who is Dr Hall?

3 Make up a headline for each of the articles. When you have finished, read out your headline and see if the others can guess which article it is for.

A

SEATTLE, May 28 (AP) — Seattle pilot Robert Mucklestone returned home nearly an hour ahead of schedule from a 23,000-mile flight that will be submitted as a record for single-engine aircraft circling the world.

Mr. Mucklestone, 49, who landed at Boeing Field Friday, took 7 days, 13 hours, 13 minutes to make the flight. Three years ago, he set a record of 12 days, 3½ hours. But that record was broken in November by Jack Rodd and Hal Benham of Cortez, Colo., who made the trip in 10 days, 22 hours.

Mr. Muckelstone's west-to-east itinerary took him from Seattle to Winnipeg, Manitoba; Gander, Newfoundland; Shannon, Ireland; Rome; Tehran; Karachi, Pakistan; Colombo, Sri Lanka; Manila; Saipan; Majuro, Marshall Islands; Honolulu; San Francisco, and Seattle.

D

AIR hostesses said yesterday that they were so tired by the end of Pan America's 12-to-18-hour long-haul flights that they were unable to look after sick passengers promptly enough or to notice minor aircraft emergencies. Today they will voice their protests in public as part of a synchronised international campaign.

"A fuse goes and you don't know about it until you start smelling it," said Miss Benedikte Kaalund, aged 32. "By the end of a flight all of us are exhausted to the point where we start missing things and can't move fast enough to do all the things we have to do."

Miss Katy Morgan, 38-year-old secretary of the British section of the Independent Union of Flight Attendants, said: "We are working harder and longer. Our inflight services and on-duty days have increased. We are concerned as human beings with these working conditions. The majority of aircraft accidents occur on take-off and landing. On long-haul flights the landing is doubly critical because of the fatigue factor."

B

A MAN armed with a toy pistol and a hand grenade who hijacked a K.L.M. jet yesterday was overpowered by a group of passengers.

The plane, a DC-9, with 69 people on board, had just taken off fro m Amsterdam Airport for Madrid when the hijacker, Paul Gooker, a 20-year-old Dutchman, demanded to be taken to Algeria.

Spanish authorities were alerted and massive security arrangements were made at Barcelona and Valencia airports.

However the captain later radioed : " The hijacker has been captured and everything is now under control."

After a two hour flight, the plane touched down at Barcelona.

Police said later that Gookel told them he was tired of living in the Netherlands

E

MALARIA is becoming such a serious hazard to travellers to hot countries that it should be made illegal for airlines and travel agencies not to warn their customers, says one of Britain's leading experts on the disease.

Airlines should be forced by law to give all passengers a pep talk, pills to protect them, and leaflets about malaria, says Dr Anthony Hall.

Travellers should be warned that a single mosquito bite can kill, or make them seriously ill. And that protection is pills taken throughout the visit and for at least a month afterwards.

"It would reduce the number of avoidable deaths in Britain," says Dr Hall, consultant physician at the Hospital for Tropical Diseases.

Malaria areas include Asia, Latin America, Central, West and East Africa, Singapore and Turkey.

The worst type is falciparum, mainly found in Africa. There were four deaths in Britain from this in the first two months of this year.

"Most deaths in Britain are due to a delay in diagnosis," says Dr Hall.

Writing in the British Medical Journal, he slams doctors for not testing returned travellers who complain of flu-like symptoms.

● British Airways and British Caledonian introduced malaria warnings to passengers earlier this year.

a pep talk: a talk encouraging people to do something
slams doctors: criticises doctors severely

C

A JAPANESE explorer has become the first man to make a solo dog sled trek to the North Pole.

The National Geographic Society said yesterday that Naomi Uemura, aged 37, reached the Pole on Sunday, after crossing more than 500 miles of the frozen Arctic Ocean from Cape Columbia on Ellesmere Island.

The National Geographic said Mr Uemura survived two attacks by a marauding polar bear ; fought his way against drifting ice and a blinding snowstorm ; and was forced to take detours around impassable ice ridges and open water during his 54-day trek.

Mr Uemura's plan to continue his one-man trip by re-crossing the Arctic Ocean and travelling down the ice-covered spine of Greenland, has been shortened because the ice is breaking up earlier than expected.

A National Geographic spokesman, Mr W. O'Neill, said Mr Uemura will be airlifted to the northern tip of Greenland where he will climb an ice mountain, nearly 10,000ft high, before attempting to become the first man to cross the island's 1,678-mile length.

NASA's Goddard Space Flight Centre is tracking Mr Uemura by a Nimbus-6 satellite which overflies the pole every 108 minutes. NASA had attributed the ice break-up to a "warm spell" that has seen temperatures in the Arctic rise to 7 degrees (minus 13C). Mr O'Neill said the temperatures at Cape Columbia were minus 58F (50 degrees Celsius) when Mr Uemura began his trip on March 7.

Mr Uemura is taking systematic snow, ice and air samples for Japan's National Institute for Polar Research and the Water Research Institute of Nagoya University.

On the fourth day of the trek, a polar bear attacked his tent and ate all the provisions. Mr Uemura killed the bear the next day when it came again and more provisions were flown into him from Cape Edward.

Mr Uemura's backers include a distillery, a manufacturer of dog food, an airline, and a sales outlet for watches.

NASA: National Aeronautics and Space Administration

59

Section B

1 By scanning the article 'Los Angeles Skytrain takes off' find the answers to the following questions as quickly as possible. Do not worry about detail that is not related to the information you are looking for.   ⇒ page 99–B.

a) Who is Freddie Laker?
b) Why was he celebrating on 26 September 1978?
c) Where did the Skytrain travel from and to on 26 September?
d) Was the flight full?
e) What happened on 26 September 1977?
f) Is the Laker flight to Los Angeles non-stop?
g) How much does the one-way trip on Skytrain cost?

Los Angeles Skytrain Takes Off

LONDON, Sept. 26 (UPI) — Sir Freddie Laker, British pioneer of cheap transatlantic air travel, launched his Skytrain service to Los Angeles today by turning up at 4 a.m. to sell personally the first ticket for the inaugural flight.

A Laker Airways spokesman said that 40 travelers, many of them American students, were lined when the Sir Freddie, 55, started the sales. He celebrated the occasion by pouring champagne for his customers and drinking a toast.

The spokesman said there were 169 fare-paying passengers and one infant aboard, plus about 50 journalists and Sir Freddie and his wife, when the inaugural flight left Gatwick Airport, south of London, on schedule at 3:05 p.m. The flight was due in Los Angeles at 8:30 p.m. local time. Normally the flight will be able to carry 345 fare-paying passengers.

The flight also marked the first anniversary of the start of the Skytrain link with New York. In its first year of operation Skytrain has flown nearly a quarter of a million passengers between London and New York and made a huge profit for Laker.

The flight to Los Angeles, aboard a DC-10, costs only $185 for the one-way trip during the peak summer season and $162 during the winter season, starting Oct. 1. It makes one stop, at Bangor, Maine, where the passengers are checked out by U.S. Customs on the flight to California.

The Laker spokesman said that while only a little more than half the 300 tickets available today had been been sold, this had been expected and he recalled that the early Skytrain flights to New York also had empty seats until travelers became accustomed to the idea of lining up for cheap travel.

Up, up and L. A.!

FREDDIE LAKER is now taking people to California for £96. When his winter rate starts on Sunday, he hopes to do the trip to Los Angeles for £84.

Skytrain really does deserve the praise it gets. Sir Freddie has broken a monopoly and made a vital service cheaper. He has done so in a candid and open way.

Laker has always said it offered fewer frills than the state airlines. If there is true competition there will be a place for more luxurious services which are also more expensive.

What matters is that we should be able to shop around. For those going to New York, and now Los Angeles, that is possible. A quarter of a million people using Skytrain in one year have made it possible!

People are voting with their money. And suddenly flights to the U.S. have become possible for those who thought such things were only for other people. That is called economic democracy.

from *Daily Express*

frills: extra services e.g. free meals

2 Look at the comment made by the *Daily Express* about Laker's Skytrain (under the headline 'Up, up and L.A.!'). Is the comment favourable or unfavourable? List the reasons which the editorial gives to support its point of view.

3 Have you ever travelled by Skytrain, or taken a charter flight? Describe briefly the advantages and disadvantages of 'cheap' flights.

4 Imagine that you have read the article and editorial about Skytrain in your newspaper. You decide to write a letter, on the subject of Skytrain and/or cheap flights in general, to the Editor of the newspaper. You can express your own views or imagine you are writing as an employee of an established airline, or as a satisfied/dissatisfied traveller on Skytrain.

Section C

1 Read the holiday adverts which follow. You have only one holiday a year. From the adverts shown, which would be your first, second and third choice? Give reasons.

2 Would your children/parents/grandparents make the same choice? Why? Why not?

3 In pairs choose one holiday. Decide what kind of information you need. Then write a letter to the organisation asking for that information.

4 In pairs act out the telephone conversation a prospective client has when he/she rings for more information. Choose any advert.

5 Which holiday do you think the following people would choose?
   a) A young adventurous couple who are not afraid of 'rough conditions', but dislike going around in groups.
   b) A retired businessman who is fond of fishing.
   c) Two students who are looking for something unusual. They have plenty of time, but money is a bit limited.
   d) A single man whose idea of a holiday is sun, rest and as little culture as possible.
   e) An 18-year-old girl who is taking her first holiday away from her family. She is fond of sport.
   f) A couple who are tired of the more conventional type holiday. They are not afraid of the unknown but are not prepared to 'rough it'.

6 Write a newspaper holiday advert based on a holiday you have had, or one which you have heard about.

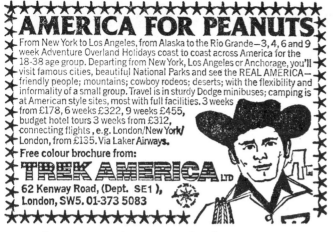
America for peanuts: visit America very cheaply

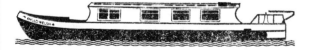
unwind: relax

10

TELEVISION ▮▮▮▮▮▮▮▮▮▮▮▮▮

Section A

1 Scan the article 'Japanese now depending on "goggle box" for many reasons' in order to answer the following questions. Work as fast as possible. Do not worry about detail that is not directly related to the information you are looking for.
⇒ page 99–B.

   a) What are the three most important possessions for the average Japanese family?

   b) How many hours per day does the average Japanese spend watching television?

   c) What is the NHK?

   d) How many families agreed to take part in the Kobe research programme on television?

   e) Why did four of the families not succeed in following the experiment for the full month?

   f) What, according to the families who took part in the experiment, were
     – the advantages of doing without television?
     – the disadvantages of doing without television?

   g) What was the conclusion of the experiment?

2 'Television now plays a big role in Japanese society not only by acting as an entertainer and informant, but also because of the grip it has on many people.' Do you think the same comment could be made about the role of television in your country?

3 What do you think would happen in your own family if you disconnected the TV? (If you do not have a TV, what changes do you think would happen within your family if you bought one?)

Japanese now depending on 'goggle box' for many reasons

IN THE mid-1960s during Japan's economic boom a colour television set became one of three "sacred treasures," with the car and air conditioner, sought by every Japanese family.

Today, nearly every family has a set with a choice of about six channels showing programmes ranging from documentaries, current events and sport to dubbed American western films, striptease and gruesome science fiction cartoons. Television now plays a big role in Japanese society, not only by acting as an entertainer and informant, but also because of the grip it has on many people.

A recent survey showed that the average Japanese spent three-and-a-half hours every day watching television, often in typically small homes where the set has been described as a "living room monster."

Japan's state-owned broadcasting corporation (NHK) said housewives are the biggest viewers. They spend an average of about five hours daily sitting on tatami (rush) matting to watch television while their husbands are working.

A major headache for parents, as in many other countries, is forcing children away from their favourite evening programmes to do their homework.

To determine the impact of television on daily life — authorities in the western city of Kobe launched an unusual experiment last October.

Impact

They sought families in the industrial city of 1.4 million people who were prepared to disconnect their sets for one month. A city spokesman said an "unexpectedly large" number of 44 families, comprising 177 people, responded.

As in Tokyo, people in Kobe are exposed to unbroken strings of television programmes from about six in the morning to the early hours of the next day.

Results of the experiments have just been released, and they give a glimpse of modern Japanese family life.

They demonstrate how much people depend on television for a variety of reasons, from news and sports reports, dramas, educational and entertainment programmes to being a substitute baby-sitter.

Four of the 44 families who agreed to the experiment failed to last the one-month course. Three of them submitted because the father was either a TV addict or failed to find another way of passing leisure time.

The other family had to abandon the experiment before the starting date because of the father's impatience.

A 30-year-old mother was quoted as saying she wanted to end a daily struggle among family members to watch favourite programmes. She also disliked dinner time being made to fit in with viewing.

Another reason was the bad effect television had on the eyes, particularly of children.

One successful case was the family of Hitoshi Fujita, a 38-year-old public servant, who put his television in a cupboard for a month and told his distraught young son that the set was out of order.

The family went to bed earlier, Mrs Fujita joined a choir and volleyball club, while her husband devoted time to reading books. As with several other successful families, the absence of television also led to more play and talk among the Fujitas.

Some families reported that dinner times were more relaxed without the pressure of television, while others said their childrens' eyesight had improved.

On the debit side, some participants said they missed their favourite programmes, while several mothers were inconvenienced by the absence of regular television timecasts, on which they relied for sending their husbands to work and children to school.

Topics

One husband, distressed by the absence of television, spent more time playing mahjong with his friends, while a father in his 30s began drinking alcohol for the first time.

Some children sometimes found themselves without anything to talk about at school, where comedians and film and singing stars are major topics during breaks between classes. The same was true for some adults.

A mother in her middle 20s said she found it hard to converse with her three-year-old child because they had no topics of common interest. Also, cartoon television programmes acted as a proxy baby-sitter for the child.

A conclusion of the experiment was that most families who turned off their television sets for one month saw the need to watch only selected programmes in future and not be governed by them.

A by-product of the experiment was that several of the participants vowed to live in future without the "living room monster." — Reuter.

mahjong: a Chinese game

4 Which of the following statements best sums up the opinion of the *Mirror* as
   expressed in the editorial comment 'Christmas Box' below?   ⇒ page 100–C.
   i)   Although it has its disadvantages, TV brings a lot of pleasure to a lot of people at
        Christmas.
   ii) In spite of the pleasure it brings to a lot of people, TV has destroyed the true
        meaning of Christmas.
   iii) It is impossible to have an enjoyable Christmas without a TV.
   iv) Those people who sneer at TV are hypocrites.

Christmas box

THE centrepiece of the family Christmas is no longer a candle-lit tree but the colour television set.

For millions of people, Christmas wouldn't have been Christmas without the telly.

Groucho Marx said TV was educational. Every time it was turned on he went into another room and read a book.

Other critics deride it for being chewing gum for the eyes. Sometimes they're right.

There IS a lot to sneer at in television. But it also brings colour and fun and memories to many — especially those living alone — who would otherwise find Christmas sad and grey.

It is a window upon the world for those to whom the alternative is a blank wall.

Like it or not, television has been THE supreme holiday attraction ever

MirrorComment

since it upstaged the cinema by showing old films.

Because of it, Morecambe and Wise are now part of everyone's Christmas. They should be shown simultaneously on both channels, like the Queen.

TV HAS reduced the religious significance of Christmas. And it HAS stopped families making more of their own fun.

But it has brought a lot of happiness, too. And only those who haven't spent hour after hour this week in front of the box have a right to deplore it.

from *Daily Mirror*

Morecambe and Wise: a popular comedy TV show in Britain
The Queen: the Queen's Christmas TV speech

5 a) List the advantages and disadvantages of television as described in the *Mirror* Comment.
   b) What is meant by the following sentences in the context of this article?
      – 'Other critics deride it for being chewing gum for the eyes.'
      – 'It is a window upon the world.'
      – 'TV has been the supreme holiday attraction ever since it upstaged the cinema.'
   c) The Comment says that television can be criticised on various grounds. Write down any words or expressions in the text which are similar in meaning to the word 'criticise'.
   d) Television is often referred to simply as TV. Find two other words for television used in the article.

6 a) Do you agree with the *Mirror*'s opinion?
   b) Write a letter to the *Mirror* in response to their Comment, saying what you think about the increasing importance of television in our lives.

Section B

1 The three articles on pages 68–9 are all in some way concerned with the problem of the growth of sex and violence on television. The articles are not however reporting the same event. ⇒ page 99–A.   By skimming very quickly over the articles decide which article is about
   a) a recently published book written by two psychiatrists;
   b) a recent survey into the attitudes of American parents towards sex and violence on television;
   c) a claim by the parents of a convicted murderer that television programmed him to kill.

2 Scan the same articles in order to answer the following questions. Work as fast as possible. Do not worry about detail that is not directly related to the information you are looking for. ⇒ page 99–B.

   ARTICLE A
   a) Who are H. J. Eysenck and K. B. Nias?
   b) Where do they work?
   c) What is the subject of the research they have been working on?
   d) What is the name of the book they have written?
   e) What did their research tell them about aggression and explicit sex on television?
   f) What did their research tell them about ordinary 'cheerful' sex scenes on television?
   g) What do they think about censorship of television programmes?

ARTICLE B

a) Which institution conducted the survey which is described in the article?
b) Which period did the survey cover?
c) What percentage of children under 18 were allowed to watch TV whenever they wanted to?
d) What percentage of children were allowed to watch any programme they wanted to on TV?
e) What percentage of children under 12 watched TV after 9 p.m.?
f) How many adults were questioned in the survey?
g) When was the last survey?
h) Had viewers' tolerance of violence increased or decreased since the last survey?

ARTICLE C

a) Who has sued three television networks? Why?
b) How old is Ronny Zamora?
c) When was Ronny Zamora convicted?
d) What was Ronny Zamora found guilty of?

A

Cut TV violence!

ROMPS WIN BUT BED EXPERTS' APPROVAL

Express Staff Reporter

TOUGHER television and film censorship is called for today by two top psychiatrists.

And they urge those in authority to pay more attention to the views of ordinary people—" rather than to those of a self-styled intellectual and artistic elite."

Professor H. J. Eysenck and Dr K. B. Nias, both based at London University's Institute of Psychiatry, spent two years researching the effects of screen sex and violence before publishing their conclusions in a book.

They say they found evidence to indicate that aggression and explicit sex in the media has an effect on attitudes and behaviour. New aggressive acts can be evoked by certain violent scenes.

But one thing they DON'T think does any harm is cheerful and enjoyable erotica—such as the film on the bedroom exploits of Fanny Hill.

They see no reason to restrict the viewing audience for that.

Pornography

The argument for censorship as given in the book, " Sex, Violence and the Media," is based on the

⟫⟫⟫→

68

point that " the portrayal of porno-graphy and violence has effects on many people which cause them to interfere with the lives, health and happiness of other people."

The two psychiatrists say it is not enough to demand a greater social responsibility from film and television producers, who are work-ing often for people whose main concern is viewing success.

" This means that some form of censorship may be essential. Such censorship already exists to some extent but it needs to be strengthened.

" No one ignorant of the facts should be allowed to pass judg-ment in matters of this kind ; the present situation of the blind leading the blind has gone on too long to be tolerable."

" We should not use censor-ship to keep criticism quiet and impotent, however much that criticism may hurt. Nothing should be banned because it is new, uncomfortable or different."

B STORRS, Conn. (UPI) — Parents who say they're worried about their chil-dren viewing too much sex and violence on television don't practice what they preach, according to a new study.

The survey, conducted by the University of Con-necticut, also said viewers do not seem to object to the growing amount of sex on TV.

The study, made by Dr. Sjef van den Berg and Dr. James H. Watt Jr., associ-ate professors of speech at UConn, checked viewers for their reactions to the 1977-78 season.

"ALMOST half of the children under 18 had no time restrictions on view-ing, and almost two-thirds had no content restric-tion," the study concluded.

In addition, nearly half of the children under 12 whose parents were sur-veyed watched television regularly after 9 p.m.

The researchers, who surveyed 220 adults, con-ducted a similar study of 180 adults during the 1975-76 season.

Viewers surveyed were less annoyed about the amount of violence shown on TV during the 1977-78 season compared to the earlier season, although many still felt there was still too much violence shown on television.

practice what they preach : do what they advise others to do

---

c 3 TV Networks Sued by Parents Of Killer in U.S.

MIAMI, May 2 (UPI)—Claiming that television programmed their son to kill, the parents of a teenager convicted of murder have sued the three major television networks for damages totaling $25 million.

The suit filed yesterday in federal court said that Ronny Zamora, 15, had "from the age of 5 years . . . been involuntarily addicted to and has been completely subliminally intoxicated by the prolonged intense viewing of tele-vision programmes distributed and televised by all three defendants . . . "

Attorney Ellis Rubin, who had defended Zamora, filed the suit on behalf of Frank and Yolanda Zamora. The suit asks for $5 million in com-pensatory damages and $10 million in punitive damages for Zamora, and $2 million in compensatory damages and $3 million in punitive damages for each of the parents.

Zamora, serving a life sentence since his Oct. 6 conviction, was found guilty of fatally shooting Elinor Haggart, his 82-year-old next-door neighbor, when she surprised him and a companion during a robbery. Mr. Rubin had argued that Zamora was insane at the time because he had become addicted to television violence and had been acting out the robbery as if it were a TV show.

3 You now have some facts from each of the articles on page 68–9. Your aim in this exercise is to find the central idea of each article. ⇒ page 100–C.

The central idea of article A is:
i)   Eysenck and Nias have published a book about sex and violence.
ii) Eysenck and Nias have spent two years at the Institute of Psychiatry researching the effects of screen sex and violence.
iii) Eysenck and Nias believe that film and television producers should show greater social responsibility.
iv) Eysenck and Nias believe that screen violence and pornography are dangerous and should sometimes be censored.

The central idea of article B is:
i)   A survey shows that parents in Connecticut are now less concerned about the growing amount of sex and violence on TV, and allow their children to spend a lot of time watching.
ii) A survey shows that nearly half of the children under 12 watch TV after 9 p.m.
iii) A survey shows that most children under 18 watch when and what they want.
iv) A survey shows that many people feel that there is too much violence on TV.

The central idea of article C is:
i)   Ronny Zamora was convicted on 6 October of shooting his 82-year-old next-door neighbour.
ii) The parents of a teenager convicted of murder have sued three TV networks for programming their son to kill.
iii) Since the age of five Zamora has been brainwashed by television.
iv) The parents of a teenager convicted of murder have won a total of $25 million compensation from three TV networks.

Section C

1 By looking through the guide to television programmes shown on page 71, answer the following questions as quickly as possible. Do not worry about information that is not directly related to the information you are looking for. ⇒ page 99–B.

BBC 1
a) What time is the local news?
b) Which sports can you watch tonight?
c) What time is the Liberal party leader speaking?
d) Which programmes after 5.40 are repeats?

BBC 2
e) Which programmes deal in some way with religion?
f) Who will Robin Ray be talking about tonight?
g) In which programme will Peter Hobday be appearing?
h) Which programmes are repeats?

ITV LONDON
i) Which programme will be given in a different language from English?
j) Who is Peter Habeler?
k) Which sports can you watch tonight?
l) Which programmes are repeats?

BBC-1

7.5 a.m.-7.55 on UHF Open University. 9.55 The Wombles, rpt. 10 Jackanory, with Geraldine McEwan, rpt. 10.15 Laff-a-Lympics, rpt. 10.35-11 The Winged Colt, episode 1, rpt. 12.40 News, Weather. 1 Pebble Mill, including Posh Nosh. 1.45-2 Bod, rpt. 3.53 (not London) Regional News. 3.55 Play School, rpt. from BBC 2. 4.20 Help! It's the Hair Bear Bunch, rpt. 4.40 Think of a Number, rpt. 5.5 John Craven's Newsround. 5.10 Out of Bounds, rpt. 5.35 The Perishers.

5 40 NEWS, WEATHER.

5 55 NATIONWIDE; and your region tonight; at 6.20 **On the Spot,** with David Steel, Liberal Party leader, facing questions from viewers.

6 55 THE BRITISH ROCK AND POP AWARDS 1978— From the Cafe Royal, London, results of the nation's "biggest ever pop popularity poll", eight awards in all. Simultaneous broadcast with Radio 1.

7 40 HAPPY EVER AFTER—Terry persuades the local operatic society to do "The King and I" with June and himself in the leading roles. Repeat.

8 10 ACCIDENT — The Figure Man. The Andrew Buchan and his chauffeur story of heavy risks and dealing. Repeat.

9 00 NEWS, WEATHER.

9 30 SPORTSNIGHT—The Greyhound TV Trophy Final from Birmingham, and The Middleweight Championship of Great Britain title-fight from the Royal Albert Hall last night between Frankie Lucas and Tony Sibson.

10 20 ARRANGEMENTS FOR EASTER—Six of our leading florists compete for the British Retail Florists Silver Rose Award at the Lyceum, London, plus a preview of the clothes designers hope we will be wearing this spring, which probably won't be half so natural.

11 05 CAMPAIGN '79. 11.45 Weather/Regional News.

BBC-2

6.40 a.m.-7.55 Open University. 10.20 Gharbar. 10.45 Parosi, rpt. 11-11.25 Play School. 2.30-4.40 Ascot Racing for the 2.45, 3.20, 3.50 and 4.25 races. 4.50 Open University.

6 55 A DEATH REPORTED—I Saw Your Light. Dr. Tom West on the death of Jesus.

7 10 FAMILY HISTORY — Gordon Honeycombe finds that the family legend's description of them as landed gentry is rubbish and that although descent from the Normans of 1066 cannot be sustained there was a John Honeycombe holding land in 1327.

7 35 NEWS, WEATHER.

7 40 THE LONG SEARCH—Rome, Leeds and the Desert. Ronald Eyre continues his religious quest. The desert is in central Spain. Repeat.

8 30 THE MONEY PROGRAMME—What has happened to sterling? Peter Hobday investigates.

9 00 SPIKE MILLIGAN IN Q8—Another selection of madness in, around or off the target.

9 30 PLAY OF THE WEEK—A Light That Shines. A first television play by Colin Tucker, a BBC producer, about a Catholic teaching order which needs new candidates. One of them is a 16-year-old boy whose mother is much against his decision. With Donald Sumpter, Steven Grives, John Wheatley and Peter Cellier. Not previewed.

10 15 ROBIN RAY'S PICTURE GALLERY—Al Capone. The first of an occasional series in which Robin Ray will compare cinema portrayals with the real thing. Five cinema versions of Capone vary in some ways, and there can't have been all those bullets on every Chicago street corner.

11 25 NEWS, WEATHER.

11 40 CLOSEDOWN — With Gwen Watford reading "History of World Languages" by D. J. Enright.

ITV London

9.30 a.m. Noddy, rpt. 9.40 The Undersea Adventures of Captain Nemo. 9.50 A Big Country: Marlin, Australian fishing. 10.20 Westside Medical, rpt. 11.10 Untamed Frontier: African Eagle. The Bataleur and Martial eagles. 11.35 England, Their England. 12 The Adventures of Rupert Bear, rpt. 12.10 Pipkins. 12.30 The Cedar Tree, rpt. 1 News. 1.20 Thames News. 1.30 Crown Court. 2 After Noon Plus. 3.20 Treasures in Store: Fasque, the house which has belonged to the Gladstone family since 1829. 3.50 Andy's Party, with Andy Stewart. 4.20 Under the Same Sun: The Enchanted Forest, rpt. 4.45 Extra-Ordinary, with Valerie Pitts. 5.15 Gambit.

5 45 NEWS.

6 00 THAMES AT 6; Andrew Gardner and the latest area news.

6 25 HELP!—Migrants Action Group, in Spanish and Portuguese.

6 35 CROSSROADS.

7 00 THIS IS YOUR LIFE—With Eamonn Andrews.

7 30 CORONATION STREET.

8 00 STREETS OF SAN FRANCISCO — Police Buff. Lucero is on trial for the murder of a police officer but gets off when a witness backs down. A court room spectator thereupon kills him.

9 00 EVEREST UNMASKED—The First Ascent Without Oxygen. Reinhold Messner and Peter Habeler reached the summit on May 8 last year having proved that it could be done without breathing apparatus, even at the ages of 33 and 35. This documentary includes film at the summit.

10 00 NEWS.

10 30 MIDWEEK SPORTS SPECIAL—The European Cup semi-finals and Nottingham Forest are still there, paired with Cologne. Plus gymnastics.

12 00 WHAT THE PAPERS SAY—with Peter Patterson on opinion polls.

12 15 CRISES → Introduced by Anna Ford. 12.20 Closedown.

from *The Daily Telegraph*

2 On pages 71–5 you can read the guide to tonight's television programmes plus a selection of reports and comments on the programmes, taken from various newspapers. Divide into pairs and imagine that you are planning the evening's viewing. You have only one television in the house so you must agree to watch the same programmes at the same time. You can watch as many programmes as you like, as long as you fit them in with the following schedule:
– You both arrive home at 6 p.m.
– You have an evening meal together lasting about half an hour.
– One person must prepare the evening meal (half an hour) and make two telephone calls (half an hour).
– The other person must do the washing up (half an hour) and write some letters (half an hour).
– You must watch at least one news programme.

TONIGHT ON BBC 1

A

Dusty . . . presenter

Top pop parade

THE Daily Star's colomnist Kid Jenson and Nationwide's Bob Wellings bring the British Rock and Pop awards 1978 to the screen tonight (BBC-1 6.55).

The five main awards are for the best single, album, male and female singers and the best group or band.

The 1979 winners will be presented with their trophies by Dave Dee, Georgie Fame, Mary Hopkin, Hank Marvin and Dusty Springfield.

These "Oscars" of the pop music world will feature Britain's favourite hits

Kid . . . host

album: record

B

Scenes to make Terry tremble ever after

TERRY FLETCHER gets himself into some chaotic situations, but any danger is usually reduced to beating Aunt Lucy to the sherry bottle.

In tonight's repeat episode of Happy Ever After (B.B.C.1, 7.40), Terry, played by Terry Scott, is bullied into presenting the local operatic society's production of The King and I.

"But you wait until the new series comes out in the autumn," says Terry. "John Kane, the writer—I could kill him—has got me doing some hair-raising things

which I tremble to read, let alone do." he said.

For a start, the lovable, bumbling Terry has to handle animals, including a grass snake, guinea pigs and a ferocious dog.

"I am petrified of snakes, the guinea pigs can give you a nasty nip," he says.

Terry Scott also suffers from vertigo.

"All I keep telling myself is that when the cameras are on me I shall be too busy remembering my lines to feel frightened, but I'm not sure I'm convinced by my own argument," he said.

hair-raising: frightening, shocking
nip: bite

C

MUM TAKES A BREAK

ACTRESS Patricia Garwood is putting her family firmly before her career.

She has taken a year off to become a full-time housewife and look after her four daughters — Amanda, 17, Tara, 14, Sasha, 11, and seven-year-old Sophie.

Patricia, 38, who stars in Accident (BBC1, 8.10) says: "I just feel that my girls come first.

"Especially the teenagers, who are now at an emotional stage of their lives and need their mother."

Patricia is married to television writer Jeremy Paul, 39, who has scripted episodes for Upstairs, Downstairs, The Duchess of Duke Street and Danger UXB.

Accident — first shown on BBC2 — tells the story of 10 people whose lives are dramatically changed by a four-car pile-up.

In tonight's episode — the third of eight — Patricia plays Dilys Martin, whose marriage is breaking up because she is incapable of having children.

D

E

ISLA ST. CLAIR: fashion and flowers.

Her heart's down on the farm

★ISLA ST. CLAIR might seem to be always up to the minute in fashion, but there is nothing she likes better than to wear old clothes and work with animals on a farm.

This week she has been in Wales making a BBC farming programme, but in ARRANGEMENTS FOR EASTER (BBC-1, 10.20) Isla hopes to give people a few ideas about what to wear and how to arrange the flowers in their homes. Six of Britain's leading florists will display their skill as they compete for the British Retail Florists Silver Rose Award at London's Lyceum Ballroom. There is also a preview of the clothes designers hope people will be wearing this spring.

Isla has promised not to turn up in her farming dungarees.

up to the minute in fashion : very much in fashion

TONIGHT ON BBC 2

F

BIG TASTE FOR HONEY

THAT debonair ex-newscaster Gordon Honeycombe has been astonished by the thousands of letters that have poured into the BBC from fascinated viewers, adding more facts and figures to the Honeycombe family legend.

In the fourth of the five programmes in FAMILY HISTORY (BBC-2, 7.10) Gordon investigates church registers to find more information about his family tree.

"There has been an enormous response to the series. In fact, I have found some cousins living near me that I didn't know about. It was a very interesting series to do."

Gordon is off to Cyprus at the end of this month to finish writing a novel called "The Edge of Heaven."

"I must really grit my

GORDON HONEYCOMBE
Interesting series.

teeth and finish the book, which is set in Cyprus. It is a love story, based on a murder which took place some time ago.

"Lately, I have been so busy that I have been rather lazy about getting to grips with writing it."

73

G

Steven breaks free of Flambards

STEVEN . . . pleased

HEART - THROB Steven Grives — flamboyant Mark in Flambards — takes on a very different role tonight.

A Light That Shines (B.B.C.2, 9.30 p.m.) takes him in exactly the direction he wants to go—towards more serious acting.

Steven plays Vivien Conroy, a sensitive older novitiate in a Catholic teaching centre.

Conroy is chosen to guide and advise a new boy, 16-year-old Stephen Fuller (played by John Wheatley).

Young Stephen was one of the most promising candidates found by Brother Martin Jerome.

Jerome (Donald Sumpter). has doubts however, when the boy seems to be at Loggerheads with all the brothers.

So he asks Conroy, who has developed an uneasy relationship with Steven to help.

Steven Grives is very pleased with the Play of the Week role, which he feels will give him a chance to break free of his Flambards type-casting.

heart-throb: idol, star

H

EVERYONE has seen Spike Milligan's zany antics on-screen.

But you should try working with him. That's really crazy !

Ask Bob Todd, who appears with Spike in Q8 (B.B.C.2, 9 p.m.).

Bob will have to watch the programme tonight to find out what was going on during filming.

"I know it sounds mad," he says. "But there's so much larking around and ad-libbing at rehearsal and during the filming that you just don't know what has been left in for viewers to see."

Ex-farmer Bob, who has been the straight man to almost all the television comedians, including Les Dawson and Benny Hill, loves working with eccentric Spike.

Surprised

" He is hysterically funny," Bob says. "But I have a reputation in the business for being a dreadful giggler, so I'm always surprised when we get through a scene without laughing.

"In last week's programme there was one part where I worried like mad that I would laugh and ruin it. But in the end, It was Spike who broke up and we had to reshoot."

One thing which

By PAT MOORE

mystifies Bob, along with the viewers, is why the programme is called Q8.

"I think it refers to Spike's Arab jokes. He turned up the other day wearing a tee-shirt with some Arabic on it.

"When I asked him what it meant he said Kuwait, but you never know with Spike," said Bob.

From his comedy appearances has come Bob Todd's first straight part.

"I'm playing an inefficient road manager in Thames TV's drama series Funny Man, with Jimmy Jewell," he says.

"It will be seen in September.

"When you've got a funny face like mine, you think you'll always get stuck in comedy roles."

I

PLAY OF THE WEEK

BBC 2, 9.30 : Enthusiastic Brother Jerome recruits 16-year-old Stephen as a candidate for his teaching order — Stephen's widowed mother, not surprisingly, is upset.

J

TONIGHT'S CHOICE
Rosalie Horner

 ROBIN RAY'S PICTURE GALLERY BBC2, 10.15 p.m.

ROBIN RAY begins an occasional series where he looks at a famous — or rather infamous—character and compares the truth with the film versions. Tonight he puts Al Capone to the test. " He is one of those attractive characters of whom everyone has heard something but whom most people know very little," says Robin Ray. Strangely enough, despite the world's best known gangster having been married at 19, none of the films mentions this fact. He died of congenital syphilis, aged 52, and not in a Hollywood-style hail of bullets.

zany: crazy, mad
larking around: having fun, making jokes
ad-libbing: improvising

74

TONIGHT ON ITV

K

Susan's dream lasts 11 years

ACTRESS Susan Hanson was signed to play in Crossroads for just two weeks. That was 11 years ago. And she is still there.

"It's been an actor's dream," says 29-year-old Susan, who plays waitress, Diane Parker. "And I don't regret a moment of it.

"I still can't believe it —the years have just gone so quickly."

But Susan thinks her dream job may finish soon. "Everything in life must end," she says. "When I have to look for other work, I may or may not be typed.

"I may be out of work —but I'll worry about that when it happens."

Susan will vanish from Crossroads in six weeks until September, while the story line sends her to America to be with her television son.

In fact, Susan will be on holiday with her husband, 30-year-old singer Carl Wayne, who has engagements in Hong Kong and Los Angeles.

Susan and Carl married five years ago, have no children and live in Twickenham, Middx.

In tonight's episode (ITV, different times) the question is whether Diane will marry Chris Hunter (Stephen Hoye), despite the opposition of his parents.

typed : stereotyped

L

M

Peek at the world

★ ON May 8, 1978, the world's greatest climbing partnership—the Italian Reinhold Messner and the Austrian Peter Harbeler—stood on the summit of the world's highest mountain and claimed the first "true" ascent of Everest.

EVEREST UNMASKED (ITV, 9.0) shows how the two climbers reached the 29,028ft. summit without oxygen equipment.

Leo Dickinson, one of the world's leading cameramen-climbers, filmed it exclusively for HTV. Filming on the summit was by Reinhold Messner. There are some breathtaking shots, too!

N CORONATION STREET

ITV, 7.30 : The more television changes the more The Street stays the same. The most popular show on the box is entering another of its periods of marriage mania.

Will Derek Wilton finally propose to Mavis Riley ? Will Brian Tilsley marry Gail Potter —could there be double wedding bells down The Street this spring ? Probably not—but it's all good for the ratings.

11

THE ARTS ▰▰▰▰▰▰▰▰

Section A

1 Scan the articles on pages 77–8 in order to answer the following questions. Work as fast as possible. Do not worry about detail that is not directly related to the information you are looking for. ⇒ page 99–B.

ARTICLE A
a) How many people did Roland Roussel kill?
b) Who did Roland Roussel intend to kill?
c) How old was Maxime Masseron when he died?

ARTICLE B
a) Why is Sherrif against belly dancing?
b) What is the attitude of the MISR to belly dancing?
c) What punishments might be introduced for – adultery; – theft; – drinking alcohol?
d) How many belly dancers are there in Egypt?
e) Who is Mrs Samya Gamal?

ARTICLE C
a) Who is Daphne Skillern?
b) What does Daphne Skillern consider to be the worst danger in pornography?
c) Does Daphne Skillern want to eliminate pornography completely?

ARTICLE D
a) Who is proposing the erection of a statue of Charlie Chaplin?
b) Which of Chaplin's films is mentioned in the article?

ARTICLE E
a) How many concerts will Jethro Tull give at London's Hammersmith Odeon in April?
b) How much will the cheapest tickets for Jethro Tull cost?

ARTICLE F
a) Who directed 'The Deerhunter'?
b) Who demonstrated outside the Los Angeles Music Centre? Why?

A CREANCES, France, Jan. 2 (UPI).—Roland Roussel, 58, confessed to using a "recipe" from one of the late Dame Agatha Christie's thrillers to poison red wine that killed his uncle and made his aunt and two others seriously ill, police said today.

Police said that atropine was the substance that Mr. Roussel, an office worker, used in the wine that killed his uncle, Maxime Masseron, 80. Atropine is described in one of the chapters in "Tuesday Club Murder."

Police said Mr. Roussel told them that his target was not his uncle or any of the other victims, but a woman friend of the family's.

C

LONDON, May 28 (AP) — Daphne Skillern, chief of Scotland Yard's war on pornography, said today that the printing of pornography in Britain is increasing so fast that the country is now a major exporter of "dirty mags."

Commander Skillern, 50, is the first woman commander of the Yard's A-3 branch, which has responsibility for obscene publications.

British magazines, she told a press conference, mostly depict "straight" pornography, and the "really nasty stuff" comes to Britain from other European countries, she said, adding: "There could be a natural progression in the British product as the porn merchants try to stay in business." She said she believes "the worst danger in pornography is the introduction of the element of violence.

"There has always been pornography and I suppose there always will be," she said. "There is no way it can ever be eliminated, but we can try to control it at a level where it corrupts the least.

"If what we now regard as pornographic becomes the normal, some people will look for something harder and it then becomes an extremely nasty business."

porn: pornography
mags: magazines

B BELLY DANCERS will soon dance for the last time in Cairo, if a group of Conservative Egyptian MPs have their way.

Some 30 parliamentarians, led by retired Air Marshal Saad El Din Sherrif, say such dancing is not Islamic and against the Koran. They would like to see it banned from Egypt for ever.

Sherrif says his proposal to ban belly dancing is being vigorously supported by the leadership of the ruling MISR party. It has also been unanimously endorsed by a parliamentary complaints and proposals committee, and there is every chance that it will become law by the end of the year.

The law against belly dancing is seen in Egypt as a test case proposal for introducing other legislation to reinforce the country's status as an important Islamic country. Such legislation would go down well with reactionary Muslim elements who believe that neither the present nor previous administrations have done enough for Islam.

Other laws under consideration could ban usury and implement the five divine laws of punishment. Included in the latter category are such punishments as crucifixion for highway robbery, stoning to death for adultery, mutila-

tion for theft and whipping, both for drinking alcohol and certain types of perjury.

Sherrif says : 'Just because I'm against belly dancing does not mean I am an extremist. For example, I have no objection to women going out of their houses for shopping or meeting their friends. But in Islam a woman is only allowed to show her face and hands in public. That is why I am opposed to belly dancing.'

The belly dancers themselves have reacted with predictable dismay to his proposal. They say his ban would kill an important art form which has taken centuries to evolve.

It would also deprive Egypt of a vital source of tourist revenue. There are some 5,000 belly dancers in Egypt alone, and the top 15, with names like Shu Shu Amin, Fifi Abdou, Nagwa Fouad and Suhair Zaki, earn £65 for half an hour's dancing.

Leading the resistance to a blanket ban is a 53-year-old Cairo housewife, Mrs Samya Gamal. Once acclaimed as the leading dancer at King Farouk's palace, Mrs Gamal is still as alert and slim-waisted as she was 30 years ago. ' I agree that some of the more overtly sexy dancing needs to be controlled, she says, ' but I don't agree it should all be banned.

D

London's councilmen are being asked to approve the erection of a life-sized statue of Charlie Chaplin in the costume that the British - born comedian made famous in his films. Councillor Illtyd Harrington, who is making the proposal, said: "We need to commemorate great Londoners, and the statue would be an inspiration to those who saw it. It

would be part of the cultural heritage of London." Claire Bloom, a close friend of Chaplin, who died early Christmas morning in his Swiss home, said that there should be a tribute to him at Westminster Abbey, burial place of British monarchs and outstanding citizens. Miss Bloom starred in Chaplin's film "Limelight."

E

JETHRO Tull, who have sold out four nights at London's Hammersmith Odeon in April, have added a fifth concert on April 14, with tickets on sale at £5, £4 and £3.

Jethro Tull: name of a rock group

F *From Wire Dispatches*

LOS ANGELES, April 10 — Two Vietnam War films, "The Deer Hunter" and "Coming Home," captured the top Oscars in the 51st annual Academy Awards last night.

"The Deer Hunter" was voted best picture of the year and won four other awards, including best direction (Michael Cimino), to lead all winners. "Coming Home" followed with three awards, including those for best performance by an actress (Jane Fonda) and actor (Jon Voight).

Meanwhile, 13 persons were arrested and five were injured in a demonstration outside the Los Angeles Music Center by members of Vietnam Veterans Against the War, who said that they were protesting the exploitation of the Vietnam War by the film industry.

2 Write headlines for each of the articles. Try to make the headlines as condensed and dramatic as possible.

Section B

1 Read the review 'A Victorian Ballad' which follows.   ⇒ page 99–B. Write down
   a) the name of the film, the director and the main actress;
   b) the name and author of the book on which the film is based;
   c) very briefly what the film is about.

2 ⇒ page 99–A. Which paragraph of the review
   a) compares the film with the director's previous films?
   b) describes Kinski's performance?
   c) tells the story of the film?
   d) describes how the director created the atmosphere of England in the last century?

3 Is the review in general favourable or unfavourable? Write down any words, phrases or sentences which the author of the review has used to praise or criticise the film.

4 If you had had the opportunity would you have liked to see this film? Why? Why not?

5 Write a newspaper review of any play or film you have recently seen. Mention what you think of
   a) the film/play itself;
   b) the acting;
   c) the direction/production.

A VICTORIAN BALLAD

Fans of "Repulsion," "Cul de Sac," "Rosemary's Baby" and "Chinatown," beware: Roman Polanski has turned his back on black humor, violence and the cinema of cruelty. Instead, with Tess, a faithful adaptation of Thomas Hardy's "Tess of the D'Urbervilles," he has made an epic film of astonishing beauty that is completely different from anything he has ever done. There is no explicit sex and none of the visual, shocking body blows we have come to expect. This slow-moving Victorian melodrama unfolds with the tragic inevitability of a Greek play in settings that could have been devised by Millais or Dante Gabriel Rossetti.

Always a perfectionist, Polanski has gone to immense trouble and expense—the three-hour film cost nearly $12 million—to reconstruct rural England of the late 1800s. Filmed in Brittany and Normandy, "Tess" is accurate down to the tiniest details:

special dwarf corn and nineteenth-century farm machinery borrowed from collectors and museums. Polanski's crew also dismantled TV antennas, buried high-tension wires and spread tons of mud to create Hardy's harsh Wessex winter.

"Tess" is about intolerance, social injus-

Kinski with Polanski on opening night: A bankable star AP

tice, and the fate of the poor at the hands of the callous rich. Polanski claims the message is universal. The very perfection of the sets, however, anchors us in the period, and the plot is quintessentially Victorian.

Tess (Nastassja Kinski), a peasant girl from apparently noble stock, is raped by Alec, a wealthy but vile seducer who has usurped the D'Urberville name. Tess flees, gives birth to a child, and marries Angel (Peter Firth), an upstanding clergyman's son who abandons her on their wedding night after learning about her past. Overcome with remorse, he returns to seek her forgiveness—but too late. Tess has become Alec's mistress to save her family from the poorhouse. When Angel reappears, Tess stabs Alec with a carving knife, runs away with her lawful husband and consummates her marriage—only to be hunted down and hanged.

Put so baldly, the plot resembles nothing so much as the mock Victorian ballad, "She was poor but she was honest, victim of a rich man's whim." But the story is not really so out of date. During the Vietnam War, for instance, countless Vietnamese Tesses sacrificed themselves to support their families, taking American lovers for whom they felt little but physical revulsion. And Polanski conveys, in ways reminiscent of Olmi's "The Tree of Wooden Clogs," the inexorable changing of seasons, the leisurely rhythm of rural Victorian England and the mindless drudgery of its landless laborers.

INNOCENT: Most impressive of all, Polanski coaxes Kinski into a performance of such depth and range that this little-known 18-year-old is bound, overnight, to become a bankable, international star. Kinski's innocent reserve and awakening sensuality in her portrayal of the young Tess are one of the film's delights. And while her suffering transforms her into a mature Ingrid Bergman-like figure, she remains an innocent to the very end, haunted and vulnerable.

Apparently, "Tess" will not be the last time Polanski changes pace stylistically. "I've always wanted to do a great love story," he says, "but I have never done the same thing twice, nor do I want to." His next film, he hopes, will be either a Western or a musical comedy. Before that, Polanski has pledged to settle his legal problems before a California court arising from a 1977 morals charge. With its tone, compassion and beauty, his new movie could almost serve as a character reference for the defense. "Tess" is, among other things, a very moral film.

EDWARD BEHR

from *Newsweek*

79

Section C

The Tut Rush

TUTANKHAMUN: THE UNTOLD STORY.
By Thomas Hoving. 384 pages. Simon and Schuster. $12.95.

In 1922, an English archeologist named Howard Carter drilled a small hole into what he hoped was the tomb of Tutankhamun. At first, he saw nothing. "But presently, as my eyes grew accustomed to the light," he wrote later, "details of the room within emerged slowly from the mist, strange animals, statues and gold—everywhere the glint of gold." His patron, Lord Carnarvon, anxiously demanded: "Can you see anything?" Carter's reply has become legendary: "Yes, wonderful things."

The wonderful things are the subject of two new books designed to appeal to the many Tut nuts. "The Gold of Tutankhamun" (by Kamal El Mallakh and Arnold C. Brackman, *332 pages, Newsweek Books, $49.95 until Dec. 31, $60 thereafter*) is lavishly illustrated, with a fairly comprehensive text. Hoving's book recounts the intriguing story of the discovery: the years spent digging without success; then the opening of the first tomb of an Egyptian pharaoh to be found virtually intact; finally the retrieval of nearly 5,000 objects.

The "untold" part of his tale mostly concerns Carter, who, as an archeologist, was both a careful excavator and an unpredictable swashbuckler. Carter, who may have pocketed a few items from the tomb for himself, always maintained that he followed proper archeological procedure on the day of his discovery, merely taking a sober look into the antechamber of the tomb. Hoving proves him an engaging liar. Together with Carnarvon and Carnarvon's daughter, Evelyn, Carter spent a magical night wandering, agog, reverent and moved, through the tomb.

'Mummy's Curse': But the bulk of the tale concerns Carter's endless bickering with the Egyptian authorities during his ten years of excavation. Carter had no sympathy for Egyptian nationalism or for the intense interest of the Arabs in the tomb; his lawyer once called the Egyptians "bandits." Carnarvon and Carter also sold exclusive rights to the story to the London Times. The rest of the press never stopped complaining, since Tut was a rich mine of stories, both gold and yellow—the yellowest being the accounts of a "mummy's curse," supposed to strike down invaders of the tomb.

Hoving can be breathless: "The reality is that, despite the camouflage, Lord Carnarvon was a brilliant man—possibly even a genius." Since the book is, in part, scholarly sleuthing, he should also have included a bibliography and more extensive footnotes. But he tells an astonishing tale cleanly and well. Why is the book still not quite right? Perhaps because the Tut story requires that rarest of writers who can do equal justice to both the ridiculous and the sublime. Evelyn Waugh should have written the parts about cultural mania, Englishmen abroad and the jackals of journalism. A great poet should describe the moment when, near the threshold of the tomb, Carter found a bouquet of ancient flowers.

—MARK STEVENS

from *Newsweek*

Tut nuts: fans of Tutankhamun
yellow: suspicious, unreliable

1   The reviewer speaks of two books. Which book does he describe in detail?

2   In one sentence say what the book is about.

3   Is the review in general favourable or unfavourable? Write down any words, phrases or sentences used by the reviewer to express his praise or criticism of the book.

4   Would you like to read the book? Why? Why not?

5   Write a short newspaper review of any book you have read.

Section D

1   Scan the article '41 survivors' in order to answer the following questions. Work as quickly as possible. Do not worry about detail that is not directly related to the information you are looking for.   ⇒ page 99–B.
a)   Where is the Michelangelo exhibition being held?
b)   How many works are being exhibited?
c)   Who lent the drawings for the exhibition?
d)   What else is on show, apart from the drawings?
e)   What did Michelangelo work on just before he died?
f)   What did Michelangelo begin to paint at the age of 26?
g)   Who was Michelangelo's great rival?
h)   Which Pope asked Michelangelo to paint the Sistine Chapel?
i)   Who was Vittoria Colonna?

2   What does the reviewer think of
a)   this exhibition?
b)   the work of Michelangelo?
Write down any words, phrases or sentences used by the reviewer to express his praise or criticism of the exhibition or of Michelangelo.

3   'The drawings were selected to display Michelangelo's progress from young prodigy to grand old master.' Briefly state the different periods represented and say which drawings represent each period.

4   Would you have liked to see this exhibition? Why? Why not?

5   Write a short newspaper review of any exhibition you have seen.

Art

41 Survivors

Michelangelo at the Morgan

All his life, Michelangelo drew indefatigably—from models, from cadavers, from memory. Yet, according to his friend Giorgio Vasari, "so that no one should ever know the extent to which he had struggled to achieve perfection," Michelangelo burned nearly all the drawings he still owned just before his death at 88. No U.S. museum has ever been able to muster even half a dozen for a show. Thus Manhattan's Morgan Library scored something of a coup when it persuaded the British Museum to send 41 Michelangelo drawings for an extended show. Superbly mounted with the understated elegance that is characteristic of the Morgan's style, the show is far and away the largest single display of Michelangelo drawings ever seen in the U.S.

The drawings were selected to display Michelangelo's progress from young prodigy to grand old master. He was only 24 when he completed the *Pietà* now in St. Peter's, only 26 when he began his famed *David* for Florence. The sketches done at this time demonstrate his incredible instinct for monumentality, acquired, as he said, with the milk of his wet nurse, the wife of a Tuscan stonecutter.

Michelangelo's next challenge was to produce a fresco in the huge new hall of the Palazzo della Signoria, to match a similar fresco to be done by his great rival, Leonardo da Vinci. Though neither painting was ever finished, the cartoons for them became, as Benvenuto Cellini recorded, "so long as they remained intact ... the school of the world"; Michelangelo's surviving sketch for a bathing soldier demonstrates why.

In mid-labor, Michelangelo was peremptorily summoned to Rome by Pope Julius II to design his tomb and later to

⟫→

paint the vaulted ceiling of the Sistine Chapel. "The place is wrong, and no painter I," grumbled Michelangelo, who considered himself first and foremost a sculptor. Three superb drawings of torsos show the pains he took over the huge scheme, which cost him four years of neck-straining labor.

By the time he was 60, and despite his success and fame, Michelangelo had turned moody, irascible, feeling himself harassed by worry and his powers waning. Yet he was already launched into the six-year labor of creating the *Last Judgment* on the altar wall of the Sistine Chapel. It was a tumultuous design, here embodied in a sketch dynamic with the swirl of falling bodies and tortured shapes of the agonized damned; his earlier calm, idealized nudes were transformed into the twisted forms expressive of his own brood-

Michelangelo's drawings: ideal head (top left); bathing soldier for lost cartoon (above)

ing sense of sin and death.

But his intimations of mortality were lightened by a series of passionate attachments to beguiling young men, chief among them Tommaso de' Cavalieri, to whom he sent one of his rare "presentation drawings." This depicts the fall of Phaëthon at the moment the overweening hero is struck down by Jupiter's wrathful thunderbolt. On it, Michelangelo wrote: "Master Tommaso, if you don't like this sketch tell Urbino [Michelangelo's servant] in time for me to make another by tomorrow evening, as I promised; and if you do like it and want me to finish it, send it back to me." Michelangelo also had his visions of idealized womanly beauty. The Morgan has a sketch of one such vision, perhaps (as some romantics would have it) a portrait of the only woman he ever loved. She was Vittoria Colonna, the Marchesa di Pescara, a woman 17 years younger than he, and their "love" seems to have been merely one of "intense spiritual friendship."

Fittingly, the show ends with drawings for the project that filled the last years of his life, the construction of St. Peter's Basilica topped by his triumphant dome. The Morgan has added memorabilia from its own stores, including maps and contemporary books. But it is the drawings that bring close that miraculous moment when Michelangelo's own hand touched paper and gave first reality to a vision.   — *A.T. Baker*

from *Time Magazine*

1   Look very quickly through the articles below and on page 85.   ⇒ page 99–A.   In one minute decide which of the articles are about
    a) the Olympics;
    b) swimming;
    c) tennis;
    d) soccer;
    e) skateboards.

2   On page 86 you will find the headlines which appeared with the articles you have just read. Match the headlines and the articles.   ⇒ page 99–A.

3   Scan the same articles in order to answer the following questions. Work as quickly as possible. Do not worry about detail that is not directly related to the information you are looking for.   ⇒ page 99–B.
    a) Which team did Celtic play against in the Anglo-Scottish cup last night?
    b) In which championship did Bjorn Borg play last night?
    c) How long did Cindy Nicholas take to swim the Channel (both ways)?
    d) In which country has skateboarding become an official sport?
    e) Where in Columbus, Ohio is the use of skateboards forbidden?
    f) How many TV networks does the European Broadcasting Union represent?
    g) Who is president of the International Olympic Committee?

4   Divide into groups. Each group is now a team of reporters responsible for producing a Saturday evening sports programme. This programme consists of sports headlines, followed by more detailed accounts of some of the week's sporting events. The programme usually describes five events and includes two or three interviews. You have already read the news content for this week (see below). Your job now is to convert it into a short lively television programme.

A

THE short-lived skateboard craze could have cost taxpayers nearly a fifth as much in hospital bills as all road accidents in 1977/78, the Department of Health and Social Security said last week.

The Department's yearly report said that one estimate for the sport — which reached a peak last Christmas and is now almost burnt out — is that it cost more than £6 millions in hospital bills.

This was set against the estimate cost of more than £50 millions for treating road accident victims in 1977/78. The report added that American and British studies suggested that skate-boarders were especially vulnerable to broken legs and head injuries.

burnt out: finished

B PARIS, April 13 (UPI) — France could be excluded from the 1980 Olympic Games in Moscow if it supports a South African rugby tour of the country this autumn, Lord Killanin, president of the International Olympic Committee, has said in a letter to the Comite National Olympique et Sportif Francais (CNOSF).

"If the CNOSF continues to give its active or passive support to the South African tour in France," the letter said, "the IOC will be obliged to apply rule 23." Rule 23 gives the IOC the right to discipline members for violations of the Olympic charter.

The CNOSF president, Claude Collard, said that his group would examine the situation at its next meeting April 24. "This question brings up the fundamental concept of the ethics of French sport," Collard said.

The French foreign minister, Jean Francois-Poncet, implied earlier this week in the French National Assembly that the South African rugby tour of France scheduled for October should not take place. He said that the government would "bring to the attention of sports federations their responsibilities on this matter."

His statement was the first move by the French government to influence the staging of the tour. Previously it has declined to intervene.

On Tuesday and Wednesday, local officials canceled the four matches that an all-white South African rugby team from the Transvaal was to have played this month at various sites in France.

C BJORN BORG'S Grand Slam bid was shattered last night when he lost in the final of the U.S. Open Championships.

He was beaten by Jimmy Connors and the same thumb injury that had forced him out of the World Championship in Dallas last May.

Connors won 6—4, 6—2, 6—2, perfect revenge for his defeat by Borg in each of the last two Wimbledon finals.

Borg, obviously hampered by the infected swelling on his right thumb, despite painkilling injections, had no answer to Connors' vicious attack.

D The nonstop two-way crossing of the English Channel has been made by only four people, all of them men. Thursday, a 19-year-old student from Ontario, **Cindy Nicholas**, became the first woman to make the two-way trip and she set a new world's record, lopping a staggering 10 hours and 5 minutes off the men's time. She swam from Dover's Shakespeare Beach to the French coast in 8 hours 58 minutes and turned around and swam back in 10 hours 57 minutes. The previous record of 30 hours was set in August, 1975, by **Jon Erikson** of Chicago, who beat his father's record by three minutes.

E MELBOURNE, Jan. 5 (Reuters).—Rocky Mattioli of Australia will defend his World Boxing Council light-middleweight title against Elisha Obed of the Bahamas in Melbourne on March 11, matchmaker **Ken Ryan** announced.

F THE European Broadcasting Union, which represents 34 television networks in Europe and North Africa, including BBC and ITV, will pay around £3,000,000 for the TV rights to the 1980 Moscow Olympics.

A spokesman for the EBU in Geneva said agreement had been reached with the Soviet authorities for a lump sum payment to cover TV rights and "basic facilities and services," including commentary positions, hotel accommodation, transport and office space.

EBU members are all Western European countries plus Algeria, Libya, Morocco, Tunisia, Israel, Jordan and Turkey. Egypt is considering joining the EBU in time for the games.

lump sum: money paid in one sum

G THIRTY people were hurt and 20 arrested when a Soccer ground was turned into a battlefield last night.

Hundreds of fighting fans stopped the Anglo-Scottish Cup tie between Burnley and Celtic.

The players went off, but the Celtic team returned later to appeal to their fans to end the chaos.

Most of those taken to hospital at Burnley had cuts and bruises. But one policeman had a broken leg.

Trouble began 13 minutes from the end of this quarter-final first leg, with the Scots trailing by a goal.

H PARIS, Jan. 5 (Reuters).— The French Sports Ministry has given its blessing to the skateboard craze, and officially designated it a sport.

The decision means that local authorities can now provide facilities for enthusiasts, who at present have to use city pavements or car parks.

given its blessing: agree to recognise it

I COLUMBUS, Ohio, March 14 (UPI) — The Columbus suburb of Upper Arlington has enacted a speed limit for skateboards.

The City Council has approved legislation to limit the speed for skateboards to 15 mph and prohibit their use on sidewalks in a business district.

The ordinance also broadens the definition for skateboards to include roller boards powered by "gravity, muscle power or mechanical motorized means."

85

¹ £3m bill for Olympics

² Soccer battle: 30 hurt

³ Jimbo blast K.O.s Borg

⁴ *Woman Swimmer Sets Channel Record*

⁵ **Skateboard Now *Un Sport***

⁶ **Title Fight in Melbourne**

⁷ *U.S. Town Sets Speed Limit on Skateboards*

⁸ *France Risks Olympic Ban In Rugby Case*

⁹ Craze cost NHS £6M

ADVERTISEMENTS

Section A

1   Read the property advertisements which follow and try to understand what the abbreviations in the adverts mean.   ⇒ page 105.

2   Read the advert 'For Quick Sale Chigwell'. By expanding the abbreviated language into full sentences, write a short paragraph describing the house advertised.

3   Choose any six of the property advertisements. Imagine that you work for an estate agent where your job is to write the publicity handouts. Write a handout based on the information you have in the advertisements, highlighting all the good points of the houses, and generally re-creating the rather extravagant style of estate agents' blurbs.

4   Below you will find a brief description of different people who are looking for accommodation. Look through the property advertisements and decide which house each family might choose to buy.

Mr Canning lives by himself and is looking for a flat. He travels by underground to work so would prefer to be near a tube station. He cannot afford more than £28,000.

Mr and Mrs Jackwell are about to retire and want to sell their London home and buy a small house or flat by the sea. They would prefer the place to be in good decorative condition.

Mr and Mrs Blakeley are looking for a house costing somewhere between £15,000 and £20,000. Mrs Blakeley has arthritis and does not like climbing stairs, so would prefer to be on the ground floor. Mr Blakeley likes gardening but after years of sharing a garden with untidy neighbours he does not want a communal garden. They have no car and no children.

Mr Blundell, who lives in the country, is tired of the long hours he spends travelling to work in London. He needs a small flat in a smart area where he can live during the week. Money is no problem.

5   Which of the houses/flats would you choose for your family?

FOR QUICK SALE
CHIGWELL
9-yr-old mod. ter. hse. in
close. 3 lge. bedrms 2 fittd
w/robes, 15ft fitted kit, 2
wcs. Full gas ch and carptd
thro'out, integ. gge. Gardens
front and rear. Excel. dec.
order £33,500 Fhld. 253
4944 day. 500 2114 after 5
p.m.

6　Read through the job adverts which follow. Choose any one of the jobs advertised and write to the address indicated, giving details of your qualifications and asking for more information.

7　Read through the theatre adverts which follow. Divide into pairs. Role-play the telephone conversation between the box office attendant and somebody ringing up to book seats. ⇒ page 105.

8　Read through the 'for sale' adverts which follow. Divide into pairs. Role-play the telephone conversation between the seller and a prospective buyer. The seller must try to persuade the person who is making enquiries to buy.

SITUATIONS VACANT

88

ENTERTAINMENT

9 Look at the 'for sale' adverts. Try to find the advert asked for as quickly as possible. Write the first word of the advert as an answer.   ⇒ page 99–B.   Which advert(s) might you reply to if

a) you have a small daughter and want to buy her a birthday present?
b) you have just had a baby?
c) you play football?
d) you are moving into an unfurnished flat?
e) your daughter wants a dolls house for Christmas?
f) you are looking for a present for your girlfriend who likes jewellery?
g) you want to learn Spanish?
h) your 9-year-old son is going skiing for the first time this year?
i) you love reading books about the Royal Family?
j) you have just bought a pair of brown shoes and need a handbag to match?
k) you are looking for a cheap piano?

ARTICLES FOR SALE

A BARGAIN. Original signed oil painting on canvas of nude, 16 x 20 inches. £15. Tel. 723 6011.

A BARGAIN. Two bottles Haig Dimple Scot Scotch whisky. £15 for this precious pair. Forest Hill area. 699 7827

ADIDAS football boots. "Beckenbauer Supers," size 42. Worn twice. Vgc. £5. Tel. 435 6713 after 6.30 pm

ALADDIN paraffin heater with 5-gallon drum with tap. Both n excellent condition. £15. 455 5145.

AN EXCELLENT 4ft. divan; Swan electric kettle; 1000w. convextor; small stainless sink; kitchen wall cabinet; modern telephone; steel locker; £15. (Will split). Potters Bar 42989.

ANKLESTRAP SHOES by Anthony de Haviland. Black suede, trimmed with silver kid. Size 4. £14. 828 8424

ANTIQUE doll, head has slight crack. Soft-bodied. Head marked 'SC England.' Would prefer to swop for boy's 9+ bike or £15. 995 6366.

ANTIQUE pine bench, £15. 01-940 6580 (Richmond).

ARMITAGE Shanks hand basin, 22¹⁄₂in x 18¹⁄₄in. Pale blue, with overlapping rim for vanity unit. Little used. Cost £40. Bargain at £15. Tel. St. Albans 73202

ART DECO brass firescreen. £15. 954 3858.

ASCOT sink water heater, £8. Mothercare safety gate, £4. 554 5045.

ASSORTED ladies clothing, size 14, to inc. dresses, skirts, coat, tops. £15. 01-555 2515 evgs & weekends.

ATTRACTIVE French double bird cage. All metal. Suitable for breeding. Removeable centre partition and nest. As new. £10. 952 0949.

AVERY Sovereign miniature scales in solid brass. Collapses into its own mahogany case and slips into picket. 5¹⁄₂in x 8in. £15. Outstanding collector's item. 821 7795.

BABY BELLING. Two rings, oven and grill. Barely used. £15. 761 1946 evs/wkends.

BABY BUGGY, made in England by McLaren. £6·0. Also Jerrycan, £2·00. Swop jerrycan for car stands. 641 0841.

BABY'S folding bath (make Precious), with foldaway changing top and lots of pockets for keeping baby items in. £2·00. Elstree area. Phone before 6 p.m. 207 1543.

CHILD'S Myers bed. Like new with detachable side panels. £15. 993 2735.

CHILDS Petite Super typewriter in case still in box. unwanted gift. ¹⁄₂ price £8. Babys pram cot sheets 5 excellent condition £2. Buyer collect. 904 7414.

CHILD'S ski suit salopette and jacket. Blue. Age 8-10 excellent condition. £15. Ring 723 0807.

CHINA SWANS five altogether £9·50. Would sell separately. Phone 937 7491

CHRISTMAS COMING. Subbuteo soccer club edition. Seven other teams, also many extras. £12 ono. Phone 958 6849 after 5 pm.

CLARKS leather wool lined high boots size 3. Handsewn silk dress, slips, jumper all new & unworn. Lot £8. Near Marble Arch. Phone 723 0623.

COATS (2), size 14, royal blue pure wool with yoke & deep pleat, and white pure wool tie belt. £15. 01-555 2515. evgs. & weekends.

COMPLETE Dolls House furniture as new £5. 200 zoo & farm animals £5. Good condition. 200 1506 (Colindale).

COPPER TANK 120 ltrs. direct supply, nearly new, plus lagging. £15. 549 3074.

COUPLE of 30in lightweight suitcases new £6 each. 554 0253 Ilford area.

CURTAIN MATERIAL Heal's large water lilies cotton print mostly green. 53 metres swop for art object etc. 722 1120 (Hampstead).

DARK GREEN maxi woollen coat, £12, s. 14. Navy blue coat (fitted) £6. s. 14 Brown woollen coat (fit girl 11 of 12 yrs. of age). 2 Skimpans-close, N. Mimms, Hatfield, Herts.

DINING CHAIRS, four, solid oak, loose lift-out seats, sound condition, £15. 01-467 8562.

DISPOSING of natural limed oak single bed complete with mattress and electric under-blanket. Excellent condition, space wanted, £15. Phone Cuffley (284) 2779 after 6 p.m.

DONEGAL tweed suit, skirt and jacket, 36 bust. Jacket would make lovely hacking jacket. £5. Telephone 274 8020.

GENTS bespoke suits in excellent condition. Owner lost weight. 38/40in. chest, 32/34in waist, 29/31in. leg. Bargain. £7 each. Phone 286 6337.

GENTS CYCLE, 27-inch wheels, fixed gear. £15. Tel. 459 4114.

GENTS golf shoes, all leather. New, by Harry Hall of Regent-st. Size 6. £12. Orpington 28342.

GENTS SARTOR gaberdine raincoat. Chest 44in. Colour fawn. A gift. Never worn £10. 28 Hanbury-rd, Acton, London, W3.

GIRLS Ski Salopettes, sizes 29in & 34in chest. £7 each. Ring after 6 p.m. 892 2695.

GOBLIN TEASMADE, as new, £10. 370 1308.

GUITAR (Welson). As new. £15. Phone 348 2894

HAND Hair Dryer and Curl-Tongs £3 each. Navy leather handbag £5. Navy skirt. M & S, size 14, worn once, £4. Rng 328 4926. i

HI-FI Unit Cabinet on castors, 2ft 9in wide x 1ft. 9in. high x 1ft. 5¹⁄₂in. deep. One adjustable shelf, 9 alternatives. Useful for files, books, etc. £15 ono. 864 3531.

HORSEHAIR MATTRESS, double size, could come in useful for home upholstery. £10. 748 7709 (Barnes area).

HUNDREDS of Autocar for sale, buyer collects. £15. W.H.Y. Telephone after 5.30. 01-886 8213.

IDEAL GIFT! "Queen Elizabeth The Queen Mother." Superb new hardback published by Country Life, with beautiful jacket. Shop price £6·50. Unopened £5 only. Phone 584 2591.

JADE, heart-shaped pendant, nearly 2in deep. 1³⁄₄in wide. New Zealand jade—looks new. Amazing bargain at £15. 741 3088.

KAFTAN, brand new, size 18-20. colour wine with gold embroideries. £15. Ring 969 1169. Friday after 7 pm. or Sunday before 11 am.

KITCHEN BASE UNIT with worktop. 3ft high, 2ft depth, 3³⁄₄ft long. £12. 435 4864 evgs or Sunday.

MOTHERCARE carrycot (brown) including chrome plated steel transporter. Good condition. Price £15 inclusive. 01-958 5996.

MOTHERCARE playpen, square, with loose padded mat. Hardly used, £12. 01-346 2358.

MUSIC VOLUME swell pedal (new)/wah wah pedal, for all musical instruments, £9·95 ono. Ring 723 7622 Room 17.

NAVY Carry Cot, stand & wheels, sheets and covers. Good condition. £9. 521 4899.

NET CURTAINS. Terylene, bought Harrods, exquisitely made, two pairs 9ft 7in. width, 9ft 12in drop, two pairs 14ft 4in width, 9ft 2in drop. £13·50 the lot. 262 2200.

NEW classical guitar bought for £28 and would only swop for a radio cassette in good working condition. 801 9201 (after 7 pm).

NEW electric Snackmaker, stainless steel combined grill hob, toaster. Swop for Burco stainless steel electric boiler. Landlord. 14 Clarendon Road, SW19. 540 7337.

NEW brown patent leather handbag 9¹⁄₂in x 7in, suede lined, edge stitched. Cost £37·50. Really beautiful bargain at £15. 352 7079.

NEW Polish linen table cloth. Buyer to collect £12. Tel 437 0385 after 6 pm.

ONE night storage heater, immaculate condition, £15. Buyer collects. Phone 01-673 3945 after 6.0 pm.

PAINTED white wood cupboard size 24in X 18in. X 6ft. £10 ono. Baby Burko wash boiler £5. Ring 698 9498 evenings.

PAIR turquoise blue curtains each 144in. wide and 86in. drop with 5 cushion covers to match, £12. Phone 739 4280.

PASTEL colour simulated mink jacket. Long sleeves, silky lining. Never worn (looks as good as real mink) bust 34in./36in. Absolute bargain. £15. 886 3775.

PEDIGREE dolls pram (collapsible) converts to carrycot, Suit large baby doll. Good condition. Bargain, £14. Phone 690 1939.

PHILIPS infra health lamp, £7·50. Vols 1-4 Medical & Health Encyclopaedia, £8. 672 4699.

PHOTOGRAPHIC reproductions, Book of U.S.A. dated 1898, £15. 800 3603. South Tottenham near Stamford Hill.

PIANO for sale. August Förster. Perfect condition except damaged leg. Must sell. £15 ono. 56 Rannoch-rd, W6.

RADIO, Marconiphone, battery/mains. Very good condition. Receives all wavelengths. Only £15. Phone 800 3603. Tottenham area.

ROCKING HORSE, Mobo, excellent condition, £5. Phone 446 0131.

from *Evening Standard*

Section B

1   The four articles below all criticise advertising, but for different reasons. Write down the particular aspect of advertising being criticised in each article. ⇒ page 100–C.

A **AN MP called yesterday for the pre-Christmas toy and sweet television commercials to be screened late at night . . . when children are tucked up in bed.**

His plea for X-rating on "kiddie ads" came as Prices Secretary Roy Hattersley announced Government plans to clamp down on advertising, especially that aimed at youngsters.

Gwilym Roberts, Labour MP for Cannock, Staffs, demanded the curbs in a bid to stop children pressurising parents into buying advertised goods.

He said: "It is a highly undesirable type of advertising.

"Children from poor families see games, toys and sweets or books promoted during early-evening programmes — then they pressurise their parents."

Mr Roberts added: "I have written to the chairman of the Independent Broadcasting Authority, Lady Plowden, asking for these advertisements to be shown only after 9pm.

MP: Member of Parliament
X-rating: for adults only

B ALMOST ONE in six of the major advertisements carried in national and regional newspapers and magazines in Britain breaches in some significant way the advertising industry's own voluntary code of practice, which demands that ads be legal, decent, honest and truthful."

Those are the first conclusions of a year-long study by the Office of Fair Trading (OFT), the consumer agency which comes under the Ministry of Prices and Consumer Protection. Prices Secretary Roy Hattersley had seen those unpublished findings when he called last week for statutory controls as "long-stop" to the industry's present voluntary regulations.

C

TOUGH new rules governing the way drink is advertised on TV are to be imposed by the Independent Broadcasting Authority.

Commercials that suggest beer makes you 'manly', that it is unmasculine not to drink, or that any particular brand of alcohol makes you more desirable — are to be banned.

D UNITED NATIONS, N.Y., May 3 (AP) — Advertising by transnational agencies and corporations can have adverse effects on developing countries, a UN study has concluded.

Released yesterday, the study said that advertising could transfer to developing countries consumer patterns of developed economies that are inappropriate to the poorer nations.

Citing no specific cases, the report also said that the lack of regulation and restrictions in developing countries could lead advertisers to make exaggerated and misleading claims for their products.

Other unfavorable results of transnational advertising, said the report, include:

● The misuse of such products as instant feeding formula for infants, which low-income groups in developing countries dilute in order to make it last longer, thereby causing malnutrition.

● The tendency of low-income groups to buy nonessential products.

● The displacement through advertising of local competition and domestic enterprises when transnational corporations do not always have substantial advantages to offer the local economy.

The report said that of the 50 largest transnational agencies, 36 are U.S.-based. Then come Japan with 10, France with 2 and West Germany and Australia with 1 each.

2   Below are the headlines which appeared with the articles. Match the headlines and the articles.   ⇒ page 99–A.

¹ TV drink ads face new ban

² How ads failed the test

³ *Transnational Advertising Faulted In UN Study of Developing Lands*

⁴ 'X'-RATING PLEA OVER KIDDIE ADS

3   Which human emotions, feelings or weaknesses are being played on in the following advertisements?

A

This is Boodles. Imported from Britain for the individual who thinks it unforgivable to make a martini or tonic drink with anything less than an ultra-refined British gin. The individual who desires incomparable pleasure that only the world's costliest methods could produce.
Yes, Boodles is expensive. But, forgivably so.

Boodles. The world's costliest British gin.

94 4 Proof Distilled From Grain General Wine & Spirits Co. N.Y. N.Y. 10022

C # How to Fight Inflation

B

GINGERSNAP

Show off your legs in our dashing city sandal! Step into the sexy look of the city sandal! So sophisticated 'n' sassy with a pleated vamp and wispy little straps that accent the curve of your ankle. Adding to the total appeal is a lean stacked heel and notched sole! Try it on—see how it lifts you up for a fresh new look! Available in white, bone, navy, amber, black smooth†; black shiny†. $32.00

sassy: saucy, smart-looking
vamp: upper front part of shoe

STEINWAY VERTICAL—HEPPLEWHITE

You are looking at a big investment.
A Steinway piano.
It takes a long, long time to build one.
And time is money.
It should be reassuring, then, to know that the money **you** invest is safe—safer than in any other piano.

D

Does your presentation look cheap?

An unimaginative folder can rob the most well-written, well-thought-out business proposal of much of its authority, because, like it or not, most people judge a book by its cover.

But you can add prestige to your presentations, reports, letters, charts, catalogs, with an Executive Presentation Folder…and Save up to 50% by buying direct.

These grained leatherette folders come in your choice of Renaissance Brown, Classic Black, Crushed Leather Brown and Walnut Grain, with matching slip-on binders.

Each holds from 1 to 50 pages, and we can even gold-stamp your trademark on each cover.... They just might be the hardest working salesmen you ever had!

4 In the advertisements shown below, the picture and/or name of the product being advertised has been deleted. From the remaining caption, decide which product is being advertised.

A "Show us this Card and we'll show you the world."

B At last. A cure for winter.

C

You can take it straight.
Or with a little plain water.
But do remember that you're tasting no ordinary ▓▓▓▓▓
▓▓▓▓▓▓▓ is a pure, single malt.
Distilled in the ancient way, in traditional handbeaten copper stills.
The result is, perhaps the finest ▓▓▓▓▓ the Highlands have to offer.
Take it slowly. Take it seriously.

D
Come with us to half the world and more. To all the beauty it has to offer. Be it in America, the Middle East or Australasia. In Europe. Or across the vast expanse that is Asia. And on the way, enjoy a standard of inflight service even other ▓▓▓▓▓ talk about. From gentle hostesses in sarong kebayas. Who'll care for you as only they know how.

E You can take our 'secretary' anywhere!

F
Come for the filter. You'll stay for the taste.

G Take a guided tour around our foundations.

H The perfect end to an awful day.

I Shop around the clock

J We'll squeeze every penny out of your lazy money.

Section A

1 Read the article 'Summer beyond wish' carefully and then answer the following questions.

   a) Where did the author live as a child?
   b) Did he enjoy the summers?
   c) How many houses were there in the village?
   d) How many roads led out of the village?
   e) In what ways was the village 'primitive'?
   f) How did the children spend their time?
   g) How did the women spend their time?
   h) How did the men spend their time?
   i) What did the author think of the programme 'Amos 'n' Andy' when he was a child?
   j) How do you know that the afternoons were particularly hot?
   k) When did the men return from work?
   l) What was the author afraid of?
   m) Where did the people sit in the evenings?
   n) Why were the children allowed to stay up one night?

2 a) Do you think that the author was happy or unhappy as a child? Underline any expressions in the passage which indicate what he thought about his childhood.
   b) The author gives the impression that life in the village was unhurried. List all the words and expressions in the passage which create this feeling of calm and slow movement.
   c) The passage describes the different parts of a typical summer day in Virginia many years ago. Although the writer says that each day was very much the same, he gives to each part of the day a particular atmosphere. Describe what that atmosphere is and list the words used by the author to create it.

3 a) Think about your own childhood. Was it similar to or very different from Russell Baker's?
   b) Would you have liked to have lived in such a village as a child?
   c) What do you think the adults in the village thought of their lives? Imagine you are one of the adult inhabitants of the village and rewrite the passage from that person's point of view.

Summer Beyond Wish

By Russell Baker

A long time ago I lived in a cross-roads village of northern Virginia and during its summer enjoyed innocence and never knew boredom, although nothing of consequence happened there.

Seven houses of varying lack of distinction constituted the community. A dirt road meandered off toward the mountain where a bootleg still supplied whisky to the men of the countryside, and another dirt road ran down to the creek. My cousin Kenneth and I would sit on the bank and fish with earthworms. One day we killed a copperhead which was basking on a rock nearby. That was unusual.

The heat of summer was mellow and produced sweet scents which lay in the air so damp and rich you could almost taste them. Mornings smelled of purple wisteria, afternoons of the wild roses which tumbled over stone fences, and evenings of honeysuckle.

Even by standards of that time it was a primitive place. There was no electricity. Roads were unpaved. In our house there was no plumbing. The routine of summer days was shaped by these deficiencies. Lacking electric lights, one went early to bed and rose while the dew was still in the grass. Kerosene lamps were cleaned and polished in an early-morning hubbub of women, and children were sent to the spring for fresh water.

This afforded a chance to see whether the crayfish population had multiplied. Later, a trip to the outhouse would afford a chance to daydream in the Sears, Roebuck Catalogue, mostly about shotguns and bicycles.

With no electricity, radio was not available for pacifying the young. One or two people did have radios that operated on mail-order batteries about the size of a present-day car battery, but these were not for children, though occasionally, you might be invited in to hear "Amos 'n' Andy."

All I remember about "Amos 'n' Andy" at that time is that it was strange hearing voices come out of furniture. Much later I was advised that listening to "Amos 'n' Andy" was racist and was grateful that I hadn't heard much.

In the summer no pleasures were to be had indoors. Everything of delight occurred in the world outside. In the flowers there were hummingbirds to be seen, tiny wings fluttering so fast that the birds seemed to have no wings at all.

In the heat of mid-afternoon the women would draw the blinds, spread blankets on the floor for coolness and nap, while in the fields the cattle herded together in the shade of spread-

OBSERVER

ing trees to escape the sun. Afternoons were absolutely still, yet filled with sounds.

Bees buzzed in the clover. Far away over the fields the chug of an ancient steam-powered threshing machine could be faintly heard. Birds rustled under the tin porch of the roof.

Rising dust along the road from the mountains signaled an approaching event. A car was coming "Car's coming" someone would say. People emerged from houses. The approaching dust was studied. Guesses were hazarded about whom it might contain.

Then — a big moment in the day — the car would cruise past.

"Who was it?"

"I didn't get a good look."

"It looked like Packy Painter to me."

"Couldn't have been Packy. Wasn't his car."

The stillness resettled itself as gently as the dust, and you could wander past

the henhouse and watch a hen settle herself to perform the mystery of laying an egg. For livelier adventure there was the field that contained the bull. There, one could test his courage by seeing how far he dared venture before running back through the fence.

The men drifted back with the falling sun, steaming with heat and fatigue, and washed in tin basins with water hauled in buckets from the spring. I knew a few of their secrets, such as who kept his whisky hidden in a mason jar behind the lime barrel, and what they were really doing when they excused themselves from the kitchen and stepped out into the orchard and stayed out there laughing too hard.

I also knew what the women felt about it, though not what they thought. Even then I could see that matters between women and men could become very difficult and, sometimes, so difficult that they spoiled the air of summer.

At sunset people sat on the porches. As dusk deepened, the lightening bugs came out to be caught and bottled. As twilight edged into night, a bat swooped across the road. I was not afraid of bats then, although I feared ghosts, which made the approach of bedtime in a room where even the kerosene lamp would quickly be doused seem terrifying.

I was even more afraid of toads and specifically of the toad which lived under the porch steps and which, everyone assured me would, if touched, give me warts. One night I was allowed to stay up until the stars were in full command of the sky. A woman of great age was dying in the village and it was considered fit to let the children stay abroad into the night. As four of us sat there we saw there a shooting star and someone said, "Make a wish."

I did not know what that meant. I didn't know anything to wish for.

from *The New York Times*

Section B

1 Read the article 'Men with a sweet smell of success' and answer the following questions. Work as quickly as possible. Do not worry about detail that is not directly related to what you are looking for.   ⇒ page 99–B.

   a) How many men are known as the 'Nose'?
   b) What is the work of a 'Nose'?
   c) What is Grasse?
   d) What is Fragonard?
   e) How old is Serge Kalougene?
   f) How old is the Fuchs' family business?
   g) What are the four main flowers used in perfume?
   h) How much does a pound of flowers cost?

2 Decide whether the following statements are true or false according to the ideas expressed in the passage. If a statement is false, correct it.

   a) Exports of French perfumes have increased in recent years.
   b) Paris fashion houses are able to continue selling their high-cost perfumes because of the huge profits gained from their sales of 'couture' clothes.
   c) Women are not employed as 'Noses', because they do not have as fine a sense of smell as men.
   d) 'Eau de toilette' is a mixture of essence and alcohol.
   e) To become a 'Nose', a man must have a good sense of smell, and a good memory.
   f) A good 'eau de cologne' never contains more than 30 ingredients.
   g) The high cost of importing flowers increases the price of the perfumes.
   h) Perfumed oil is a mixture of flowers, pork and beef fat.

Men with a sweet smell of success

FORTY men in a French town near the Mediterranean are each known as The Nose.

They are courted, spied upon and even lured with attempted bribes.

For it is upon the sensitivity of their noses that one of France's most important industries depends . . . perfume.

The 40 "Noses" in the sun-washed, hill-fringed town of Grasse create the essences of perfume that have made France the world's biggest manufacturer and exporter of sweet smells, with exports up by 20 per cent. recently.

FASHION

There is no room for women, who do not win such important positions in the male-dominated region of Provence.

With the market for hand-made couture clothes limited, big name Paris fashion houses now support their luxury operations largely on sales of perfume. Veteran fashion house Nina Ricci, for example, has been given new life in recent years by a best-selling perfume.

Virtually all the essence of big name perfumes is created by the picturesque perfume factories of Grasse, which date from the Middle Ages.

Perfume makers buy the essence and mix it with water for eau de cologne or eau de toilette, or with alcohol for perfumes at their gleaming new factories near Paris.

The "Nose" at Fragonard, one of Grasse's biggest essence factories, is 35-year-old Serge Kalougene.

Patrick Fuchs, president of the 200-year-old family business, sighed at how his competitors were constantly trying to lure his "Nose" away.

Sitting in his laboratory, M. Kalougene was surrounded by about 4,000 bottles filled with one or more of the four principal flowers used in perfume—lavender, jasmin, rose and orange flower — plus materials with interesting odours such as orange peel, rosewood, sandalwood, pepper, ginger, bay leaf, basil, mint and even tobacco.

BOTTLES

He said : " After I add an ingredient I smell the mixture and then I add more. It is like music, or cuisine.

" Then I submit the essence to a perfume distributor to consider. If they want it heavier, or fresher, I can change it."

M. Kalougene became a "Nose" because he had developed a good sense of smell " and a good memory for the thousands of products that go into perfumes. So far, I have put 27 ingredients into just one essence for men's eau de cologne and there will be a total of 60."

EXPENSE

In the fields around Grasse grow the flowers that feed the factories. The flowers are one reason why perfume is so expensive.

It takes 2,200 pounds of orange flowers to make two pounds of essence of orange flower. The flowers cost nearly £5 a pound.

The cost further mounts in the processing : flower petals picked at dawn and trucked to the factory are "cooked" by steam in huge copper vats and the essence distilled under pressure. Other flowers are cooked with pork and beef fat which absorb the floral odours and become perfumed oil.—UPI.

Reading skills

A Skimming or reading to identify the subject matter

We skim when we want to get a quick general idea of what a large piece of reading material is about. We skim, for example, when we look through a book in a bookshop before deciding whether to buy it or not. We also skim when reading a newspaper. Most of us do not read the whole of a newspaper in detail. We tend first to look through it quickly to get an idea of the day's news before selecting those articles or parts of the newspaper we wish to read in detail. This initial survey is skimming. Although most of us are fairly used to doing this in our native language, we seem to have a block when it comes to doing the same thing in another language, very often because most of the reading we have done in a foreign language has consisted of the slow, careful, detailed reading of fairly short passages. A number of the exercises in this book are designed to give practice in skimming over a long passage or a number of shorter passages. Sometimes you are asked to match headlines with their articles, sometimes to identify the article or articles which deal with a certain subject or theme. Your aim here is to find the answer as quickly as possible. You are not concerned with the ideas or conclusions of the writer. You should not be at all worried about words you do not know nor about details such as dates, names or figures *except* where such details might help you to identify the subject matter. For example, in an exercise which requires you to find the article which goes with the headline 'Pope to visit China' you should first run your eye over the articles to see if any contain the words 'Pope', or 'China', or words connected with them, e.g. the Church, the Vatican, Rome, Peking, Chinese officials etc. Once you catch sight of a relevant word or phrase in an article, focus your attention on that article long enough to make sure that it really matches the headline. (There may, for example, be more than one article on the Pope or on China, but probably only one that connects them.) Do not attempt to read the article in more detail at this stage, but continue with the exercise. With a little practice you should be able to complete a skimming exercise within 60 seconds.

B Scanning or reading quickly to find specific information

Scanning is the reading skill we use when we want to find the answer to a specific question. We use it when we look up a word in a dictionary, when we consult an encyclopaedia or the index of a reference book, when we look up a telephone number or the time of the next train to Liverpool. We also use it when reading a newspaper – to find out the football results, the name of the newly elected President, the time of a television programme or the temperature in Madrid. In all these cases we are not concerned with understanding the whole article or text but only with locating one item of information.

In a scanning exercise, read the first question carefully. Decide what form the answer to the question is likely to take. For example, if the question is asking for the name of a person or a town, you will need to look for initial capital letters. If it is asking for a date, you will need to look for figures. In other cases be prepared to stop at key words relevant to the information you are looking for. Once you know what you are looking for, run your eyes very quickly over the article or group of articles. Work as fast as you can. Do not stop over parts of the material that are not directly related to what you are looking for and do not get distracted at this stage by ideas or information you may otherwise be interested in. Once you have found the relevant part of the passage, read more slowly and more carefully until you find the specific piece of information required. Stop and note down the answer. Do not continue reading the passage at this stage. Go on to the next question in the exercise.

C   Reading for the central ideas

Whereas skimming and scanning are both fairly superficial kinds of reading, reading for the central ideas implies that we are willing to give a text more of our attention. Here we are interested in understanding more fully what the writer is trying to convey. We are not however necessarily concerned about all the details of the passage and we do not have to read slowly in order to arrive at the main ideas.

Some of the exercises in this book are designed to train you to find the central ideas of a text rapidly. When doing these exercises, try to read slightly faster than you normally do, not so fast that you completely lose the sense of what you are reading, but not slowly enough to take in all the minor details. Do not waste time and energy on trying to remember dates, figures and names. Remember that you are looking for the writer's main thoughts and conclusions.

D   Guessing the meaning of words

When reading the articles in this book you are likely to meet a number of words and expressions which you do not know. Do not react to this either with a feeling of despair or by rushing to the nearest dictionary. Remember first that it is not always necessary to understand every single word in order to understand the article, and secondly that it is often possible to work out the meaning of a word you have never seen before. Below are a number of strategies which help in the task of guessing words you do not know.

- Look at the context of the word. Look at the words which come before and after it. Is the word used as another way of stating or describing something that has already been stated or described? Does the writer go on to explain what he means by the word? (A writer often says the same thing twice in order to get his point over.)
- See whether the word occurs elsewhere in the text. Its meaning in another sentence may be clearer, or by looking at the same word in different sentences you may find it easier to guess the meaning because you have more clues.
- Look at the kind of word it is – noun, adjective, adverb etc. What function does it have in the sentence? How does it relate to the other words in the sentence?
- Look quickly to see whether you can split the word up into parts you know. Take for example the word 'unbearable'. You may never have seen this word before,

but if you break it down into its parts un-bear-able you will quickly understand its meaning. The prefix 'un' describes the absence of a quality. Bear is a common verb. The suffix 'able' adds the sense of something that must or can be done, in this case something that can be borne. Familiarity with the more common prefixes and suffixes greatly helps in guessing words. However, once you have worked out a word in this way always check that it makes sense in the context of the passage.

Reading skills practised

Reading skill practised	Relevant chapter or section in the book e.g. 3 = Chapter 3 1(B) = Chapter 1, Section B	Advice
Skimming	1(A), 2(A,B), 3(A), 4(A), 5(B), 6, 7(A), 8(A), 9(A), 10(B), 11(B), 12, 13(B)	Page 99
Scanning	1(B), 3, 4(A,B,C,D), 5, 6, 7(B), 8(A,C), 9, 10, 11(A,B,D), 12, 13(A), 14(B)	Page 99
Reading for the central ideas	3(B), 4(A), 10(A,B), 13(B)	Page 100
Guessing the meaning of words	2(B), 3(A,C), 4(D), 5(B), 8(B)	Page 100
Understanding headlines	1(A), 2(B)	Page 102
Understanding advertisements	13(A)	Page 105

Follow up work

WRITTEN WORK

Writing newspaper articles	1(A)
Writing newspaper headlines	3(B), 9(A), 11(A)
Writing advertisements	5(A), 9(C), 13(A)
Writing letters	6, 7, 8(A), 9(B,C), 10(A), 13(A)
Writing a review	11(B,C,D)
Writing narrative	4(E)

ORAL WORK

Discussion	4(B,C,D), 5(A), 6, 7, 8(A,B), 10(A,C)
Role play	9(C), 13(A)
Producing a radio programme	3(A), 5(B)
Producing a television programme	12

Headlines

The special language of newspaper headlines is one of the major problems faced by learners of English when they begin to read English newspapers. There is, however, a clear pattern in that special language and, once the rules have been understood and the key words mastered, a lot of the difficulty disappears.

A headline writer has to keep two principles in mind. First he must attract the attention and interest of the reader. Some newspapers are more sensational than others, but even the so-called 'serious' newspapers use fairly dramatic language in their headlines. Secondly, the headline writer is influenced by the fact that in a very limited space he must give the reader some idea of what the article is about. The result is a language characterised by

a) a very condensed structure;
b) words chosen for their brevity and/or their dramatic quality;
c) the use of cultural allusions or associations ranging from the latest TV show to quotations from the Bible.

Features (a) and (b) of headline language are practised in the book, and below is a short description of the main differences between the grammar of headlines and that of ordinary English, and a dictionary of headline words. Feature (c) is not specially exemplified or practised in the book.

The structure of headlines

1 Articles and the verb 'to be' are frequently omitted, e.g. MAN HELD; COMPANIES MORE CHEERFUL.

2 The verb system is greatly simplified.
   - The present simple tense is used to describe something happening in the present or the past, e.g. WOMEN DRIVE BETTER THAN MEN CLAIMS REPORT; DYNAMITE KILLS 52 (meaning '*killed*').
   - The present simple tense is used to describe both something happening now, and something which happens repeatedly, e.g. US VISIT TESTS THE POPE AS POTENTIAL WORLD LEADER.
   - The present progressive tense is sometimes used, mostly to give the meaning of something that is developing. The auxiliary is omitted, e.g. RAIL CHAOS GETTING WORSE.
   - The infinitive is used to refer to the future, e.g. POPE TO VISIT U.S., TV TO AID THE DEAF.
   - In passive constructions the auxiliary is omitted and only the past participle is used, e.g. QUEEN TOLD OF DRINK AT BOYS SCHOOL; HIJACKER ARRESTED.

3 A series of nouns used as adjectives are blocked together, often without any verbs or conjunctions, e.g. SHOTGUN DEATH RIDDLE DRAMA; PAY ROW BLACKOUT THREAT; SOCCER BOY RAIL VICTIM.

The vocabulary of headlines

Headline word	Meaning	Example
ACCORD	agreement	WAGES ACCORD REACHED
*AID	help	MAN AIDS POLICE
*AXE	cut, destroy, take away	LABOUR AXE COLLEGES IN TORY TOWNS
BACK	support	UNIONS BACK PEACE MOVE
*BAN	prohibition	BUS BAN ON PUPILS AFTER ATTACK ON CREW
*BAR	exclude, prohibit	SOUTH AFRICA BARS TEAM
*BID	attempt	NEW PEACE BID IN RHODESIA
*BLAST	explosion	POLICE IN LONDON PROBE BLAST
*BLAZE	fire	FAMILY DIES IN BLAZE
BLOW	injury/disappointment suffered	CARTER POLL BLOW
*BOOST	help, incentive	INDUSTRY GETS BOOST
*CLASH	dispute, violent argument	STRIKERS IN CLASH WITH POLICE
COUP	revolution, change in government	GENERALS OUSTED IN COUP
*CURB	restraint, limit	NEW CURBS ON IMMIGRATION
*CUT	reduction	BIG CUTS IN AIR FARES
DEAL	agreement	PAY PITS DEAL HOPE
*DRIVE	campaign, effort	PEACE DRIVE SUCCEEDS
ENVOY	diplomat	AMERICAN ENVOY TAKEN HOSTAGE
*EXIT	leave	EXIT ENVOYS IN RACE STORM
GEMS	jewels	ACTRESS LOSES GEMS
GO-AHEAD	approval	GO-AHEAD FOR DEARER GAS
GUNMAN	man with gun	GUNMAN RAIDS 3 BANKS
*HALT	stop	CHANNEL TUNNEL HALT
*HAUL	large quantity which has been stolen and later discovered	CANNABIS HAUL
*HEAD	lead, direct	BUCHANAN TO HEAD PEACE MISSION
HELD	retained, kept in custody	MURDER: TWO MEN HELD
HIT	affect badly	FUEL STRIKE HITS HOSPITALS
JET	aeroplane	THREE KILLED IN JET PLUNGE
JOBLESS	unemployed	NUMBER OF JOBLESS INCREASES
KEY	essential, vital	KEY WITNESS DIES
*LINK	connection	MAFIA LINK SCANDAL BREAKS
MAN	representative	CARTER MAN IN CHINA
NET	total	DRUG RAID NETS £1 M
ORDEAL	painful experience, drama	JAIL ORDEAL ENDS
OUST	push out, drive out, replace	ARGENTINA OUSTS UNION LEADERS
OUTPUT	production	INDUSTRIAL OUTPUT INCREASES IN ITALY
PACT	agreement, treaty	PITS PACT ENDS
*PAY	wages, salary	PAY RISE FOR MINERS
PIT	coal mine	PIT TALKS END

PLEA	request for help	'FREE CHILDREN' PLEA
*PLEDGE	promise	LABOUR PLEDGES HIGHER PENSIONS
*PLUNGE	steep fall	DOLLAR PLUNGES
POLL	election, public opinion survey	SWEDISH POLL SHOWS SWING TO RIGHT
PRESS FOR	demand, ask for	TEACHERS PRESS FOR PAY RISE
*PROBE	investigate	NEW VACCINE TO BE PROBED
QUIT	leave, resign	WILL CARTER QUIT?
*RAID	attack, robbery	£23½ M DRUG RAID
RIDDLE	mystery	GIRL IN SHOTGUN DEATH RIDDLE
*ROW	argument, dispute	BBC BOSS QUITS IN ROW
*SCARE	public alarm	RABIES SCARE HITS BRITAIN
*SPLIT	divide	NATIONALISATION SPLITS PARTY AT CONFERENCE
*SQUEEZE	shortage, scarcity	PETROL SQUEEZE AHEAD
STORM	angry reaction, dispute	MP'S RACIST SPEECH STORM GROWS
STRIFE	conflict	INTER-UNION STRIFE THREATENS PEACE DEAL
*SWITCH	change, deviation	DRAMATIC SWITCH IN INCOMES POLICY ANNOUNCED
*SWOOP	sudden attack or raid	DRUG SWOOP IN MAYFAIR
TALKS	discussions	PEACE TALKS THREATENED
TOP	exceed	POST OFFICE PROFITS TOP £40 M
*VOW	promise	WOMAN VOWS VENGEANCE
WALKOUT	strike (often unofficial)	FACTORY WALKOUT THREAT OVER SACKING
WED	marry	FINANCIER FREE TO WED

* can be found in headlines as a noun or a verb with this meaning.

Advertisement abbreviations

Property advertisements

Abbreviation	Meaning	Abbreviation	Meaning
avail.	available	kit.	kitchen
balc.	balcony	lnge.	lounge
bed.	bedroom	lrge.	large
c.h.	central heating	min.	minute
col.	coloured	mod.	modern
com.	communal	o.n.o.	or nearest offer
cond.	condition	pkg.	parking
cpts.	carpets	prop.	property
ctns.	curtains	p.b.	purpose built
dble.	double	recr.	recreation
dec.	decorated	sep.	separate
fit.	fitted	shwr.	shower
flr.	floor	sngle.	single
gdn.	garden	stn.	station
gge.	garage	terr.	terraced
inc.	including		

Entertainment advertisements

adm.	admission
avail.	available
bkble.	bookable
bkgs.	bookings
cont.	continuous
dly.	daily
evgs.	evenings
exhib.	exhibition
inc.	including
mat.	matinee (afternoon performance)
perf.	performance
progr.	programme
sep.	separate
wk.	week

Answers

1 News in brief

Section A

1 1 – D 2 – B 3 – F 4 – M 5 – G 6 – I 7 – K 8 – J 9 – C 10 – E 11 – L 12 – A.
3 hit – harmed, affected; haul – seizure, find; pledge – promise; blaze – fire;
plea – request, demand.
4 1 A dispute about jobs may affect a children's hospital. 2 Profit from crime exceeds £166
million. 3 A mother's request for her son fails. 4 A young wife attempts to conquer her
fear. 5 Some schoolchildren have been forbidden to travel by bus after a crew was
attacked. 6 An actress marries. 7 Heroin worth £1 million has been seized.
6 1 – E 2 – F 3 – A 4 – G 5 – B 6 – C 7 – D

Section B

1 a) Singapore. b) Because they threw away cigarettes he gave them. c) Senator Edward
Kennedy. d) Off North East Malaysia. e) A postal clerk. f) John Hopkins University.
g) 130 metres. h) 40 i) Nuclear Regulatory Commission.
2 a) False ('He backed it for the first time.') b) False ('Householders may keep the
equipment.') c) False ('Their boat capsized in heavy seas.') d) True e) False ('Because
their cooling systems may be unable to withstand earthquakes.') f) True g) False
('Christmas commemorative stamps.')

2 Home news

Section A

1 a) B b) A c) E d) C e) A f) A,F g) A h) B,C,E i) A,D,F
2 a) True b) False (Sets will cost at least one third more.) c) True d) False (Mr Bates was
working his first day.) e) False (The burglars escaped.) f) False (Mr Bates was out.)
g) False (MPs are demanding a statement on plans for juggernauts.) h) False (An American
professor had forecast an epidemic.) i) False (They stopped work to make tea as part of
their action for a pay rise.) j) False (Doctors fought to save his leg.)

Section B

1 a) A young soccer fan has been a victim on the railways. b) Television is going to help deaf
people. c) A pet plan has been approved. d) There was a storm in a tea cup. e) MPs are
going to fight a plan about juggernaut lorries. f) The manager of a hotel tricked a gunman.
2 See articles on page 15.
3 1 – E 2 – A 3 – B 4 – C 5 – F 6 – D
4 a) iv b) iii c) i d) i e) i f) iv g) iii

3 Foreign news

Section A

1 a) F,J b) A,H c) G d) D,K,L e) A,B,C,E,F,H,L f) C,K,L
2 a) Her dolphinarium in Clacton was destroyed in a storm. b) 1,073. c) Leningrad.
d) He pulled a knife on a policeman. e) −36.5°C. f) In retaliation for university police
actions against a student demonstration. g) 26,687. h) 180 million lire. i) Yes. j) 13
years ago. k) To study the distribution of space dust near the Earth's surface. l) A bishop
beheaded by Roman soldiers in 305.

Section B

1 ARTICLE A
a) 20 b) USSR

ARTICLE B
a) If no new cases are discovered before October next year. b) Outbreaks were isolated by
vaccinating in a ring around the affected village. c) The nomads are constantly moving.
d) So that even the most isolated people knew what smallpox looks like.

ARTICLE C
a) Once a year. b) They tried to stop the ships carrying the hunters leaving
Newfoundland. c) The police smashed the padlocks with hammers. d) They were picked
up by coastguards.

ARTICLE D
a) Director of Amnesty's British Section. b) There are harsh laws against terrorism. c) Mr
Ahmed Ben Bella.

ARTICLE E
a) The existence of small hotel and motel operations in the USA. b) From theft. c) Senior
vice president of Rocky Pomerance Association. d) There may be 40,000 to 50,000
unreturned hotel keys in circulation at any time.

2 A iv B ii C i D i E ii
3 The original headlines were: ARTICLE A – Treaty against use of weather in warfare goes into
effect. ARTICLE B – Smallpox conquered this time say doctors. ARTICLE C – The seal
savers go to war. ARTICLE D – Amnesty cites 110 countries. ARTICLE E – Towel stealing
is least worry of crime-menaced US hotels.

Section C

1 a) Texas prison. b) The wildest of men are thrown into the same arena with the wildest of
animals, i.e. men attempt to ride wild or untamed horses. c) Four – real cowboys,
newcomers to Texas, ex-prisoners, average everyday people. d) Five Sundays. e) Hot –
80°F. f) A prisoner completing a 30-year sentence. g) He came sixth.
2 a) ii b) i c) i d) iv e) ii f) iv g) i

4 Business news

Section A

1 A iii B i C ii D iii E ii
2 1 – B 2 – C 3 – E 4 – A 5 – D
3 ARTICLE A
a) Since 1963. b) 124. c) Seven days. d) No. e) Their card numbers are flashed onto a board in the local Key Market. f) £5,000. g) 12 weeks. h) From normal promotional expenditure.

ARTICLE B
a) A liberal research group that monitors inflation among necessities. b) By 4.8%.
c) 70%.

ARTICLE C
a) Fujitsu Fanuc of Japan. b) Programmed pick-and-place mechanical arms and hands.
c) Up and down, rotates on its own axis, backwards and forwards horizontally. d) Robots are inevitable and Wellings wants his company to be in at the beginning.

ARTICLE D
a) The great grandson of the younger brother of Friedrich Engels. b) A textile factory.
c) The family mansion. d) A housing project. e) 250.

ARTICLE E
a) To find mistakes in the US Government payroll. b) 29. c) 600. d) He was not on the payroll and the maximum federal salary is half that paid to Donald Duck.

Section B

1 a) 56. b) One in three. c) A counselling group. d) Six. e) To recognise their talents.
f) An independent cleaning contractors consisting of four women.
2 a) False (She is 56 and recently got a divorce.) b) False (It is paid for by a State grant.)
c) False (There have been moves in Congress to set up similar centres in all states.)
d) True e) True

Section C

1 a) Microprocessors. b) Pollution, the energy crisis, the bomb. c) Government, political, trade union and industry representatives. d) 29. e) That thousands of new products will emerge from the microprocessor revolution but there will not be massive unemployment.
f) That service industries would continue to absorb people displaced. g) It can dispense cocktails. h) A loss of jobs resulting from loss of international competitiveness.

Section D

1 a) A newsletter. b) Cameras. c) Rent-a-thief. d) The inventor of Sentry II. e) The lie detector. f) A research paper. g) 48 miles per hour.
2 a) iii b) ii c) iii d) iv e) ii f) iv

5 Technology and science

Section A

1   LIFT-OFF
a) Anser Electronica, Ltd.   b) Sao Paulo.   c) Police and civilian motorists.   d) $100 or $110.   e) Motoring magazines.

DISAPPEARING INK
a) Paper Mate Division of the Gillette Company.   b) Boston, Massachusetts, USA.
c) Everybody, particularly students and secretaries.   d) $1.69.   e) Any newspaper or magazine.

VOICE OF CONSCIENCE
a) Carole Kiebala.   b) Palatine, Illinois, USA.   c) People who want to lose weight.
d) About $10.   e) Health, slimming or womens' magazines.

TRIPLE TELECAST
a) Sampo Corporation.   b) Tapei, Taiwan.   c) Television fans, television critics.
d) $900.   e) TV magazines.

TALKING SCALES
a) The American Foundation for the Blind.   b) New York, USA.   c) Blind people, hospitals.   d) $1,000 for the Detecto institutional scale; $100 for home bathroom scale; $150 for the thermometer.   e) Specialist magazines for the blind, medical journals.

SUPER DROPPER
a) Apex Medical Supply.   b) Bloomington, Minnesota, USA.   c) Parents, nurses.   d) 79 cents.   e) Medical journals, magazines for parents.

COMBATING SPILLS AT SEA
a) David Usher.   b) Detroit, Michigan, USA.   c) Oil companies, port authorities.
d) Price not stated.   e) Industrial magazines.

EARLY-WARNING SYSTEM
a) Lawrence Electronics.   b) Bradford, England.   c) Car owners and drivers.   d) About the same price as a good quality car radio.   e) Motoring magazines.

JOGGERS' PACESETTER
a) Majima Co. Ltd.   b) Tokyo, Japan.   c) People who like playing sport, particularly runners.   d) $40.   e) Sports magazines.

2   LIFT-OFF describes an inflatable air bag used to lift or jack up cars.

DISAPPEARING INK describes a ballpoint pen that writes at any angle and uses ink which can be erased.

VOICE OF CONSCIENCE describes a battery powered device which will warn anybody who opens the fridge against eating.

TRIPLE TELECAST describes a television with three screens to enable the viewer to watch three channels at once.

TALKING SCALES describes bathroom scales which call out the user's weight.

SUPER DROPPER describes a precisely calibrated medicine dropper that enables the user to dispense an accurate amount of liquid medicine.

COMBATING SPILLS AT SEA describes a system of work platforms which enable salvage crews to unload oil tankers in heavy seas.

EARLY-WARNING SYSTEM describes a radar system mounted on the front of a car and connected to a dashboard instrument which warns a driver of obstacles up to 300 feet ahead.

JOGGERS' PACESETTER describes a battery-powered device which looks like a wrist-watch and emits a steady 65 decibel beeping tone that helps a runner regulate his or her stride.

Section B

1 1 – C   2 – F   3 – B   4 – E   5 – A   6 – D
2 a) The late 1950s.   b) Chief solar forecaster for the Space Environment Services Center. c) Trees are bent over by some mysterious force.   d) For evidence of tampering or trickery.   e) *Nature*.   f) Thousands of kilometres.   g) It should be five times its present sum.   h) At the centre of our nearest active galaxy, M87.   i) Their gravity is so powerful that no radiation can escape from them.
3 a) False (Voyager-I has discovered the ring and photographed it.)   b) True   c) False (She thinks they could be a triggering factor.)   d) False (Mr Gretz thinks it unlikely.)   e) True f) False (One film was taken by a surveyor.)
4 a) iii   b) iv   c) i   d) i   e) iii   f) iv   g) ii

6 Comment

1 a) Editorial C   b) Editorial A   c) Editorial B

2 1 – B   2 – A   3 – C

3 EDITORIAL A
a) The decision by the Anglican clergy to reject the proposal to have women priests.   b) The Editorial agrees with the Anglican clergy on the grounds that the ordination of women would hinder Christian re-unification.

EDITORIAL B
a) The decision by prison officers to begin disruptive tactics in pursuit of an overtime claim, and the rebellion of inmates at Gartree prison.   b) Overcrowding in prisons should be reduced by finding methods other than imprisonment for dealing with many classes of criminals. More money should be spent on the treatment of law-breakers.

EDITORIAL C
a) The World Bank's annual meeting.   b) The rich countries of the world should increase the help they give to the poor countries.

4 EDITORIAL A
a) Those women who want to enter the priesthood.   b) Christian re-unification.   c) The Womens' Liberation movement.

EDITORIAL B
a) Keep order, uphold the law and punish wrongdoers.   b) Three to one.   c) Prison officers at 30 or 40 places will begin disruptive tactics.   d) Maximum security prisons.   e) Britain. f) In the 19th century ('Victorian architects').   g) They become hardened and confirmed criminals.   h) Rapists – imprisonment; habitual drunkards – a half-way house between imprisonment and freedom with a firm but supportive regime; young violent offenders – a glasshouse regime where they are kept away from confirmed criminals; con-men – not imprisonment but a punishment where the wrongdoer has to give back to society what he/she has taken.

EDITORIAL C
a) The opportunity to improve the chances that new-born infants will survive and that the quality of their lives will improve.   b) Last week.   c) 800 million.   d) President of the World Bank.   e) 2000 million.   f) 36 years.   g) Life expectancy has increased, literacy has doubled, more children go to school, one family out of every four has a safe water supply. h) Access to markets and capital.

7 Letters to the editor

Section A

2 a) 'Benefits of smoking.'   b) 'Where can we teenagers go?'   c) 'What a carry on for our working mums.'   d) 'Good sense from a Russian prison.'   e) 'The shame of hanging.' f) 'Year of the child.'

Section B

I

Letter	In answer to letter or article	Name of previous writer	Subject matter	Agree/Disagree
A	Letter	Young man	Life in the Services	Agree
B	Article	Judith Simons	Pop music performers	Disagree
C	Article	David Haworth	Abortion	Disagree
D	Not stated	Jill Tweedie	Alcoholism	Disagree
E	Not stated	Dr Alice Heim	Experiments on animals	Agree
F	Letter	Not stated	Arming the police	Disagree

8 Motoring news

Section A

I   1 – E   2 – C   3 – D   4 – F   5 – B   6 – A

2   ARTICLE A
a) 40%.   b) Place de la Concorde, Paris.   c) None.   d) Restaurant proprietors.

ARTICLE B
a) A generation ago.   b) Critics of radar.

ARTICLE C
a) Volvo.   b) 800.   c) If the lights are left on after parking.

ARTICLE D
a) At least 84.   b) Rewinding a meter.

ARTICLE E
a) Transportation Secretary.   b) $50 billion.   c) Engine repair.

ARTICLE F
a) Students.   b) They opposed it.   c) The ban would affect tourism and visitors.

4   a) False (The government is planning to make seat belts compulsory.)   b) False (Delegates refused to vote on the direct issue.)   c) True   d) True   e) False (Lord Lucas thinks that compulsion hits at the fundamentals of democracy.)

Section B

1 a) iii b) ii c) i d) i e) iv f) iii g) iv h) iii i) ii j) iv
2 a) True b) False (A catering manager pointed to a pie with genuine pride.) c) False (He is Bulmer's Cider chairman.) d) False (The Government has accepted the main recommendation.) e) True f) False (The committee recommended changes in the price of petrol, and the provision of banks and picnic spots.) g) True

Section C

a) Boys at Shrewsbury School. b) Throughout the Common Market. c) Minister for the disabled. d) Invashrew. e) Head of craft and design at Shrewsbury School. f) The British Steel Group, The Ministry for the disabled, and the EEC.

9 Travel news

Section A

1 a) D b) A c) B d) E e) C

2 ARTICLE A
a) Robert Mucklestone. b) November.

ARTICLE B
a) Madrid. b) He wanted to go to Algeria because he was tired of living in the Netherlands.

ARTICLE C
a) Japanese. b) 1,678 miles. c) every 108 minutes. d) 7 March.

ARTICLE D
a) 32. b) Secretary of the British section of the Independent Union of Flight Attendants.
c) On take-off and landing.

ARTICLE E
a) Falciparum. b) Consultant physician at the Hospital for Tropical Diseases.

3 The original headlines were:
ARTICLE A – US man circles world in 7 days. ARTICLE B – Passengers overpower jet hijacker. ARTICLE C – Japanese reaches Pole on dog sled. ARTICLE D – Airline girls 'too tired to cope'. ARTICLE E – Taking the bite out of malaria.

Section B

1 a) British pioneer of cheap transatlantic air travel. b) He was launching his Skytrain service to Los Angeles. c) London to Los Angeles. d) No. e) The Skytrain link with New York began. f) No. g) $185 during peak summer season and $162 during the winter season.
2 Favourable: Skytrain has broken a monopoly; it has provided a vital service cheaper; we are able to shop around.

Section C

5 a) 'Black Mountain Trekking Holidays', 'Indian Summer' b) 'Spectacular fishing and hunting resort in Quebec' c) 'Indian Summer' d) 'Greek island villas' e) 'Ski-easy'
f) 'China' or 'Be a houseguest in France'.

10 Television

Section A

1 a) A colour television set, a car and an air conditioner.   b) 3½ hours.   c) Japan's state-owned broadcasting corporation.   d) 44.   e) Three families stopped because the father was a TV addict, or failed to find another way of passing leisure time. One family stopped because of the father's impatience.   f) ADVANTAGES: the family went to bed earlier; some parents began other hobbies; there was more play, talk and communication among the families; the childrens' eyesight improved; the end of the daily struggle within the family over which TV programme to watch; dinner times were more relaxed.   DISADVANTAGES: people missed their favourite programmes; mothers were inconvenienced by the absence of regular TV timechecks on which they relied for sending their husbands to work and children to school; some men spent more time out of the home (e.g. drinking); children and adults found themselves out of the general conversation; one mother had nothing to say to her child; mothers missed the baby-sitter aspect of TV.   g) Families who took part in the experiment saw the need to watch only selected programmes in future and not be governed by them.

4 i

5 a) ADVANTAGES: it brings colour and fun and memories to many people, especially those living alone; it brings people into contact with the outside world.   DISADVANTAGES: it is rather like a drug; it has reduced the religious significance of Christmas; it has stopped families making more of their own fun.

b) 'Other critics deride it for being chewing gum for the eyes' – other people criticise television for being like a drug; we watch it mechanically without really appreciating it but nevertheless needing it. 'It is a window upon the world' – it brings people into contact with what is happening outside their homes. 'TV has been the supreme holiday attraction ever since it upstaged the cinema' – TV has been the most important holiday attraction ever since it took over from the cinema as the most popular form of entertainment.

c)   deride, sneer at, deplore.   d) the telly, the box.

Section B

1 a) A   b) B   c) C

2 ARTICLE A
a) Psychiatrists based at London University's Institute of Psychiatry.   b) London University's Institute of Psychiatry.   c) The effects of screen sex and violence.   d) *Sex, Violence and the Media*.   e) They have an effect on attitudes and behaviour.   f) They are not harmful.   g) Some censorship may be essential but censorship should not be used to keep criticism quiet and impotent.

ARTICLE B
a) The University of Connecticut.   b) 1977–78 session.   c) Almost 50%.   d) Two thirds.   e) Nearly half.   f) 220.   g) 1975–76.   h) Decreased.

ARTICLE C
a) The parents of Ronny Zamora. For programming their son to kill.   b) 15.   c) 6 October.   d) The murder of an 82-year-old woman.

3 A iv   B i   C ii

Section C

1 BBC1
a) 55.5 and 11.45.   b) Greyhound racing and boxing.   c) 6.20.   d) 'Happy ever after', 'Accident'.

e) 'A death reported', 'The long search', 'Play of the week'.   f) 'Al Capone).   g) 'The money programme'.   h) 'Parosi', 'The long search'.

ITV LONDON
i) 'Help!'   j) He climbed Mount Everest without breathing apparatus.   k) Football and gymnastics.   l) 'Noddy', 'Westside medical', 'Rupert bear', 'The cedar tree', 'Under the same sun'.

11 The arts

Section A

1   ARTICLE A
a) One.   b) A woman friend of the family's.   c) 80.

ARTICLE B
a) Because it is not Islamic and against the Koran.   b) Unfavourable.   c) Adultery – stoning to death; theft – mutilation; drinking alcohol – whipping.   d) 5,000.   e) A former leading belly dancer at King Farouk's palace.

ARTICLE C
a) The commander of Scotland Yard's A-3 branch which has responsibility for obscene publications.   b) The introduction of the element of violence.   c) No.

ARTICLE D
a) Councillor Illtyd Harrington.   b) 'Limelight'.

ARTICLE E
a) Five.   b) £3.

ARTICLE F
a) Michael Cimino.   b) Members of Vietnam Veterans against the War. They were protesting about the exploitation of the Vietnam War by the film industry.

2   The original headlines were: ARTICLE A – French killing is linked to Christie novel.   ARTICLE B – Egypt may forbid all belly-dancing.   ARTICLE C – British official says porn trade becoming big.   ARTICLE D – No headline.   ARTICLE E – More Tull.   ARTICLE F Academy awards.

Section B

1   a) Tess of the D'Urbervilles (film), Polanski (director), Nastassja Kinski (main actress).
    b) *Tess of the D'Urbervilles* by Thomas Hardy.   c) Intolerance, social injustice and the fate of the poor at the hands of the rich. The story of a peasant girl who has an illegitimate baby, and is subsequently rejected by her husband and who is finally hanged for the murder of her seducer.
2   a) One. b) Six. c) Four. d) Two.
3   The review is favourable: 'an epic film of astonishing beauty'; 'always a perfectionist, Polanski has gone to immense trouble'; 'Tess is accurate down to the tiniest details'; 'the very perfection of the sets'; 'most impressive of all . . . international star'; 'with its tone, compassion and beauty'.

Section C

1   *Tutankhamun : the untold story.*
2   The book describes the events preceding and following the discovery of the tomb of Tutankhamun, with particular emphasis on the part played by the archeologist Carter.
3   In general favourable. FAVOURABLE COMMENTS: 'He tells an astonishing tale cleanly and well.' UNFAVOURABLE COMMENTS: 'He should also have included a bibliography'; 'Why is the book still not quite right?'; 'Evelyn Waugh should have written the parts about cultural mania, Englishmen abroad and the jackals of journalism'.

Section D

1   a) At Manhattan's Morgan Library.   b) 41.   c) The British Museum.   d) Maps and contemporary books.   e) He painted the dome of St Peter's Basilica.   f) 'David'. g) Leonardo da Vinci.   h) Pope Julius II.   i) The Marchesa di Pescara 'perhaps the only woman Michelangelo ever loved'.
2   a) Excellent: 'far and away the largest single display of Michelangelo drawings ever seen in the US'; 'superbly mounted'.   b) He considers him a genius: 'his incredible instinct for monumentality'; 'the miraculous moment'.
3   His instinct for monumentality shown by drawings for the Pieta and for David; the painting of a fresco in the Palazzo della Signoria (sketch of a bathing soldier); painting of the Sistine Chapel (three drawings of torsos); painting of 'The Last Judgement' in the Sistine Chapel (a sketch dynamic with the swirl of falling bodies); series of passionate attachments to young men (a drawing sent to Tommaso de Cavalieri showing the fall of Phaethon); the construction of St Peter's Basilica (drawings for this project).

12 Sport

1   a) B,F   b) D   c) C   d) G   e) A,H,I
2   1 – F   2 – G   3 – C   4 – D   5 – H   6 – E   7 – I   8 – B   9 – A
3   a) Burnley.   b) US Open Championships.   c) 19 hours 55 minutes.   d) France.   e) On the sidewalks of a business district of Upper Arlington.   f) 34.   g) Lord Killanin.

13 Advertisements

Section A

2   This is a 9-year-old modern terraced house situated in a close. There are three large bedrooms with two fitted wardrobes, a fitted kitchen which is 15 foot long, and two toilets. It has full gas central heating and is carpeted throughout. There is a garage, and there are gardens at the back and front of the house. The house is in excellent decorative order and the freehold costs £33,500. Telephone 253 4944 during the day or 500 2114 after 5 p.m.
4   Mr Canning – Fulham S.W.6;   Mr and Mrs Jackwell – Hove;   Mr and Mrs Blakeley – Walthamstow; Mr Blundell – W.2 Pied-a-terre.
9   a) Child's petite super typewriter, Complete dolls house furniture, Pedigree dolls pram. b) Baby buggy, Baby's folding bath, Mothercare carrycot, Mothercare playpen, Navy carrycot etc.   c) Adidas football boots.   d) An excellent divan, Baby Belling, Curtain material, Dining chairs, Kitchen base unit, etc.   e) Complete Dolls House furniture.   f) Jade heart-shaped pendant.   g) Three Walker's pre-recorded language courses.   h) Child's ski suit.   i) Ideal gift.   j) New brown patent leather handbag.   k) Piano for sale.

Section B

1 A – TV advertisements aimed at children.   B – Advertisements which break the voluntary code of practice demanding that advertisements be legal, decent, honest and truthful. C – Advertisements suggesting that it is desirable and manly to drink.   D – Advertising by transnational companies in developing countries.
2 1 – C   2 – B   3 – D   4 – A
3 A – snobbery;   B – sex;   C – snobbery and desire to be rich;   D – need to impress others with smart appearances.

14   Features

Section A

1 a) In a crossroads village of northern Virginia.   b) Yes, very much.   c) Seven.   d) Two. e) There was no electricity or plumbing and the roads were unpaved.   f) Mostly outside – fishing and looking at and playing with animals.   g) Working in the house and in the afternoons they slept.   h) Working in the fields during the day and in the evening they escaped to the fields to drink whisky or sat on the porch talking.   i) It was strange to hear voices coming out of furniture.   j) The women drew the blinds and spread blankets on the floor for coolness. The cattle herded together under the trees to escape the sun.   k) With the setting sun.   l) Ghosts and toads.   m) On the porches.   n) Because a very old woman was dying.
2 a) He was happy: 'I enjoyed innocence and never knew boredom'; 'I did not know what that meant. I did not know anything to wish for.'
b) 'a dirt road *meandered* off'; 'afternoons were *absolutely still*'; 'far away over the fields the *chug* of an ancient steam-powered threshing machine could be *faintly* heard'; 'Then – a big moment in the day – the car would cruise past'; 'The stillness resettled itself'; The men *drifted* back'.
c) MORNING: time for getting up early and working (early morning hubbub of women). AFTERNOON: a drowsy, sleepy part of the day, when the main housework was over and the only sounds to be heard were those of nature (heat, nap, escape the sun, absolutely still, bees buzzed, birds rustled).   EVENING: Time of relaxation (men drifted back, laughing too hard).   NIGHT: mysterious, the sounds of the countryside again become important (lightening bugs, a bat swooped, I feared ghosts, I was afraid of toads).

Section B

1 a) 40.   b) They create the essences of perfume.   c) A town (in the south of France) containing perfume factories.   d) One of Grasse's biggest perfume factories.   e) 35.   f) 200 years.   g) Lavender, jasmin, rose and orange.   h) Nearly £5.
2 a) True   b) False ('big name Paris fashion houses now support their luxury operations largely on sales of perfume'.)   c) False ('There is no room for women, who do not win such important positions in the male-dominated region of Provence'.)   d) False ('It is a mixture of essence and water.')   e) True   f) False ('I have put 27 ingredients into just one essence for men's eau de cologne and there will be a total of 60.')   g) False (The flowers are not imported.)   h) True